To Al Gain'
My friend
Oscar Poole
4-16-10

To Al Geiner
Great times
My Best Regards
Kyle 10
4/14/10

# There's Only One Oscar Poole

*Entrepreneur*
*Statesman*
*Theologian*
*Philosopher*

## Taking Pork Back to Washington for 13 Years

An Autobiography
by Oscar Poole
In His Own Words

22241 Pinedale Lane • Frankston, Texas 75763
903-876-3256 • www.hiddenmysteries.com

2009

# There's Only One Oscar Poole
## Oscar Poole
(2009)

All Rights Reserved
TGS Publishers

No part of this book may be reproduced or transmitted in any form or by any means, graphic, electronic, or mechanical, including photocopying, recording, taping or by any information storage or retrieval system, without the permission in writing from the author and/or publisher.

TGS Publishers
22241 Pinedale Lane
Frankston, Texas 75763
903-876-3256

www.HiddenMysteries.com
info@hiddenmysteries.com
Printed and bound in the USA.

www.OscarPoole.com
oscarpoole@aol.com

Printed and bound in the USA.

# Table of Contents

**Meet Oscar Poole** ............................................................................. - 13 -

**Foreword** ........................................................................................... - 15 -

**Endorsements** .................................................................................. - 19 -

**Chapter I The Life of Col. Dr. Oscar Poole** ................................... - 23 -
    A modern day Entrepreneur -Statesman-Theologian-Philosopher ........ - 23 -
    Personal note ......................................................................................... - 23 -
    Why this book? ...................................................................................... - 23 -
    A spiritual journey ................................................................................. - 24 -
    Added note ............................................................................................ - 25 -

**Chapter II The Times of My Birth** .................................................. - 27 -
    Tourist environment .............................................................................. - 28 -
    Eclectic .................................................................................................. - 28 -
    A funny story ......................................................................................... - 28 -
    O.M. Poole ............................................................................................ - 29 -
    That South Georgia food! ..................................................................... - 29 -
    More on my dad .................................................................................... - 29 -
    Conservative values of O.M. Poole ...................................................... - 30 -
    My own conservative values ................................................................. - 32 -
    Waiting for the cotton to be unloaded ................................................... - 33 -
    Homemade ice cream and boiled peanuts ............................................. - 33 -
    The ferry boat ........................................................................................ - 33 -
    The Poole historical "claim to fame"! ................................................... - 34 -
    The Baptist Sunday school .................................................................... - 35 -
    My church connections ......................................................................... - 36 -
    Billy Brown ........................................................................................... - 37 -
    Georgia red clay .................................................................................... - 37 -
    Milking cows ......................................................................................... - 38 -
    The roar of the Atlantic Ocean .............................................................. - 39 -

German submarines ........................................................................ - 39 -
Uncle Denny and Mrs. Farrell ...................................................... - 40 -
A vision at age 5! ......................................................................... - 41 -
Another word about Billy Brown .................................................. - 41 -
Sally Geanette Cain Poole ........................................................... - 42 -
Preachers were my heroes ......................................................... - 44 -
Once we had an accident ............................................................ - 45 -
Summary ..................................................................................... - 45 -

## Chapter III Grammar School ...................................................... - 47 -
The alphabet ................................................................................ - 47 -
The advent of Billy Brown ............................................................ - 49 -
Don't forget Breece McCray ........................................................ - 49 -
Next to the moon! ........................................................................ - 49 -
My piano debut ............................................................................ - 50 -
Helen Keller ................................................................................. - 51 -
The bombing of Pearl Harbor ...................................................... - 51 -

## Chapter IV Junior High .............................................................. - 53 -
My first paying job ....................................................................... - 53 -
Church pianist .............................................................................. - 54 -
Victor Gray and O.H. Ferdon ....................................................... - 55 -
My first views of solar energy ..................................................... - 56 -
My camp meeting days ............................................................... - 56 -

## Chapter V High School .............................................................. - 59 -
My first car ................................................................................... - 59 -
T.C. Wilder arrives! ..................................................................... - 60 -
Don't forget Harold Tumblin and Charles Mueller! ..................... - 61 -
Football! ....................................................................................... - 61 -
Senior year finally arrives! ........................................................... - 62 -
My dance orchestra experience .................................................. - 62 -
The Nazarenes ............................................................................ - 63 -
Tension ........................................................................................ - 65 -

    Time to get serious about college ................................................................ - 66 -
    The summer of 1947 ........................................................................................ - 66 -
    One date in high school ................................................................................ - 67 -
    Mary Jane Snodgrass ..................................................................................... - 67 -
    Summary ............................................................................................................. - 68 -

## Chapter VI My College, University Years ................................................ - 69 -
    Here comes the shock of my life ................................................................ - 70 -
    Homesick for two weeks ............................................................................... - 72 -
    The "A" in Greek ............................................................................................... - 72 -
    A college music professor at age 18! ......................................................... - 72 -
    My first snow! .................................................................................................. - 73 -
    Time for the Christmas holidays .............................................................. - 73 -
    Diversion for an excursion .......................................................................... - 76 -
    AT-ONE-MENT! ................................................................................................. - 78 -
    Let's back up — return 60 years ................................................................. - 78 -
    Back at Trevecca .............................................................................................. - 79 -
    Breaking news from home! .......................................................................... - 79 -
    Back to Trevecca (Nashville, 1949) ............................................................. - 80 -
    My sophomore year in college .................................................................... - 81 -
    Marriage to Edna — June 2, 1950 ............................................................... - 83 -
    Our honeymoon ................................................................................................ - 84 -
    It's 1950 ................................................................................................................ - 84 -
    John B. Stetson University ............................................................................ - 85 -

## Chapter VII Graduate School ........................................................................ - 87 -
    My first church, First Church of the Nazarene, Clarkson, Kentucky ............... - 88 -
    High School Glee Club .................................................................................. - 88 -
    Head-on confrontation with raw fundamentalism ............................... - 90 -
    Edna, her clothes, her hair, her rings ........................................................ - 90 -
    Always look for the positive! ...................................................................... - 92 -

## Chapter VIII Age 27 — The Baptists! ......................................................... - 95 -
    A new church building ................................................................................... - 96 -

The Oscar Poole Evangelistic Association ........................................... - 97 -
Back to Seminary ................................................................................ - 97 -
The Elizabeth Baptist Church, 1960-61 .............................................. - 98 -

## Chapter IX Methodists Calling — Age 31 .................................. - 101 -
The Casselberry Community Methodist Church ............................... - 101 -
Something's not right ........................................................................ - 102 -
The Laconia Church .......................................................................... - 103 -
The Larchmont Church of God, 1963 ............................................... - 104 -
The President Harry S. Truman story ............................................... - 104 -
First Methodist Church, Oakfield, New York, 1964–1967 ................ - 107 -
A special service forever to be remembered! ................................... - 109 -
The Cabin on Sodus Bay (The Piano Story) ..................................... - 113 -
The God-is-Dead Series ................................................................... - 114 -
Other tidbits at Oakfield .................................................................... - 115 -
Michael and his chocolate milk ......................................................... - 115 -
"You can have anything you want!" ................................................... - 116 -
The E. Stanley Jones experience ..................................................... - 117 -

## Chapter X The Texas Excursion ................................................... - 121 -
An interlude of two years, 1967-69 ................................................... - 121 -
So, off we go! .................................................................................... - 121 -
Our opening service .......................................................................... - 124 -
When you create a new goal ............................................................ - 125 -

## Chapter XI Back To The Methodists ............................................ - 127 -
A word about tension and conflict ..................................................... - 127 -
Pastoral visitation .............................................................................. - 128 -
Operation Involvement ...................................................................... - 129 -
Lordy, Lordy, Oscar turns 40! ........................................................... - 130 -
A traumatic experience — Box died! ................................................ - 131 -
Back in Georgia, 1970 ...................................................................... - 132 -
Over half-way, 1970 .......................................................................... - 133 -

## Chapter XII Gilmer County — 1971-75 .................................................. - 135 -
    Doing … then writing ........................................................................ - 138 -
    The school of music ......................................................................... - 140 -
    My doctorate .................................................................................... - 141 -
    The charismatics ............................................................................. - 144 -
    Added note to problem-solving ........................................................ - 145 -
    Meanwhile, back at the ranch ......................................................... - 146 -

## Chapter XIII Thomaston, Georgia — 1975 ............................................ - 149 -

## Chapter XIV Chatsworth — 1977-79 .................................................... - 151 -
    One of the Bishop's favorites .......................................................... - 151 -
    La Vie is born! 1978 ........................................................................ - 154 -
    On the road again! .......................................................................... - 156 -
    The Jim McDonald Story ................................................................ - 157 -
    1980 ................................................................................................. - 158 -
    The Alturas United Methodist Church ............................................ - 159 -
    I "saw" a note .................................................................................. - 161 -
    The church flourished ..................................................................... - 162 -
    New move and it is glorious! ........................................................... - 164 -
    Snowball .......................................................................................... - 166 -

## Chapter XIV Charleston, West Virginia ............................................... - 173 -
    Another false direction ................................................................... - 174 -

## Chapter XV The Next Three Years ...................................................... - 179 -
    Are we there yet? Almost! 1986-89 ................................................. - 179 -
    Guidance comes! ............................................................................ - 179 -
    The truck is loaded (and so is the cat) ............................................ - 182 -
    The bamboo church ........................................................................ - 183 -
    "They've got my idea!" .................................................................... - 184 -
    The Wendell Cross story ................................................................ - 186 -
    La Vie returns! ................................................................................. - 189 -

## Chapter XVI The Promised Land ............................................................... - 193 -
 (Col. Poole's Georgia BAR-B-Q, Inc.) ........................................... - 193 -
 The Voice .................................................................................. - 194 -
 Pat Buchanan for President ........................................................ - 198 -
 The FORMAT changes! .............................................................. - 200 -
 "A Rhema Word" ........................................................................ - 202 -
 Testimony ................................................................................. - 202 -
 Back to the BAR-B-Q saga ......................................................... - 204 -
 Meditation ................................................................................. - 205 -
 "What concerns you?" ................................................................ - 205 -
 "I want you to write it down!" ...................................................... - 209 -
 My Magna Carta ........................................................................ - 211 -
 Calling things ............................................................................ - 215 -
 Pat Buchanan ........................................................................... - 216 -
 Our "Day of Infamy" ................................................................... - 217 -
 Long Beach, California ............................................................... - 218 -
 Where did the name PIG HILL-OF-FAME come from? ................. - 219 -
 A few words from Edna .............................................................. - 220 -
 A theology for BAR-B-Q .............................................................. - 221 -
 The John Baeder painting .......................................................... - 222 -
 The Washington D.C. story ........................................................ - 224 -
 How do you explain .................................................................... - 226 -
 We want to keep this family legend going ................................... - 226 -
 Why do I stay involved in politics? .............................................. - 227 -
 A summary of the BAR-B-Q experience ...................................... - 227 -
 The media ................................................................................. - 229 -
 Here's the media we attracted .................................................... - 229 -
 More attraction — famous people! .............................................. - 233 -
 The Law of Association .............................................................. - 235 -
 Five years as Chairman, Gilmer GOP ......................................... - 235 -
 The 1996 Convention in San Diego ............................................ - 236 -

More on the yellow suit ............................................................................. - 237 -
2007 .......................................................................................................... - 238 -
Surprise! .................................................................................................. - 238 -
The 2000 Convention in Long Beach ...................................................... - 239 -
The 2004 Republican Convention in New York City ............................... - 239 -
Disappointed ............................................................................................ - 240 -
The Atlanta Airport .................................................................................. - 242 -
Arrival ...................................................................................................... - 242 -
Orientation ............................................................................................... - 243 -
Why did we go to the RNC? .................................................................... - 244 -
A statement of JOY! ................................................................................ - 244 -
Media list (2004, New York City event) ................................................... - 245 -
The bus trip ............................................................................................. - 248 -
Some concluding observations ................................................................ - 249 -
2009 .......................................................................................................... - 251 -

## Chapter XVII A New Career ................................................................ - 255 -
The McCutchen-Poole Small Business Coalition .................................... - 255 -
Legacy ..................................................................................................... - 256 -
Our way of life is threatened ................................................................... - 257 -
Free enterprise vs. socialism ................................................................... - 258 -
Free market control vs. government control ........................................... - 259 -
More on the McCutchen-Poole Small Business Coalition ....................... - 261 -
Speaking of a Voice in America .............................................................. - 263 -
Talk Radio ............................................................................................... - 263 -
Gilmer County a Model ........................................................................... - 263 -

## Chapter XVIII Summary ........................................................................ - 265 -
Personal Legacy ..................................................................................... - 267 -

## Addendum I New Insights Gained from Listening ............................. - 269 -

## Addendum II Secrets of Success ........................................................ - 275 -

THERE'S ONLY ONE

**Addendum III My Take On The Dalton Conclave** .................................- 281 -
   (Out-of-the-Box and Off-the-Wall) ...............................................................- 281 -
   Elohim ...........................................................................................................- 284 -
   Back to the Dalton Conclave ........................................................................- 285 -

**Addendum IV McCutchen-Poole Small Business Coalition** ................- 289 -
   Breaking News! .............................................................................................- 293 -

**Addendum V Letter From Gilmer County Commissioners** ...................- 295 -

**Addendum VI Letter From Gilmer County,
              Georgia Chamber of Commerce** ........................................- 296 -

**Addendum VII Letter From Mayor, East Ellijay Georgia** ......................- 297 -

**Addendum VIII Tribute From the U.S. Senate in the Congressional Record** .........................................................................................................- 298 -

**Addendum IX Letter From Lt. Governor Casey Cagle** ..........................- 299 -

**Addendum X Card From Senator Saxby Chambliss** ............................- 300 -

**Other Works by Col. Poole** .......................................................................- 301 -

Lester Maddox in Oscar's Model A

Dr. Reginald Johnson and Oscar

Oscar and Edna's Home

THERE'S ONLY ONE

Pat and Shelley Buchanan

# Meet Oscar Poole

Colonel Oscar Poole, along with his wife, Edna, is the highly successful owner of Col. Poole's Georgia BAR-B-Q, Inc., located 75 miles north of Atlanta on Highway 515 in the little town of East Ellijay. It is home to the Taj-Ma-Hog, the Hog Rock Café, and the world famous Pig-Hill-of-Fame.

He is also president of La Vie, an international retreat center, located near Blue Ridge, Georgia.

THERE'S ONLY ONE

Col. Poole is an experienced pastor, having served for 22 years in the United Methodist Church. He was chosen "Minister of the Year" three times and his ministry was once selected as one of the "One Hundred Most Creative and Innovative" in the denomination. Presently, he is a member of the National Association of United Methodist Evangelists.

In 1996 he was a delegate to the Republican National Convention in San Diego, where he played the piano for two occasions.

His international experience includes travels to Holland, Israel, Lebanon, Egypt, Jordan, Mexico and Haiti. He has made ten trips to Brazil, where he has spoken and played the piano to audiences in most of the major cities.

He is co-founder and active promoter of the McCutchen-Poole Small Business Coalition, the purpose of which is to enlist the 27 million small businesses in America to become a viable force in addressing political reform (see www.oscarpoole.com).

# Foreword

By Edna Y. Poole

I have been married to Oscar Poole for 59 years! I agree with Reggie Johnson and Joe McCutchen — there's only one Oscar Poole!

Oscar says he plans to live to be 124! Should that be true, I'll have to be around to 122, because he couldn't make it without me!

A "rags-to-riches" story, Oscar literally "fell" into a roadside business, a shack by the side of the road, with a "negative capital" of $35,000, which today is known in many circles world-wide as a serious American business. Oscar's *conservative principles* got him where he is today, along with his hard work, and mine!

This book by Oscar begins with the "times" (or history) of the southern United States into which he was born. He reveals his *conservative* background.

Oscar takes us through his public school days, through college and university and beyond. He takes us on a *spiritual pilgrimage* as a successful pastor until he and I opened the famed BAR-B-Q restaurant alongside Highway 515 in East Ellijay, Georgia, in 1989.

# THERE'S ONLY ONE

From 1989 to 2009 the book takes the reader through an almost *celestial* journey of how ONE MAN (with me at his side) with a strong SPIRITUAL UPBRINGING, conservative business principles, and a passion for the AMERICAN FREE ENTERPRISE system — and his desire to share the American Dream, OVERCAME obstacles and adversities to achieve one of America's great success stories of our modern era.

At the end of the book the reader will note the "McCutchen-Poole Small Business Coalition" in which Mr. McCutchen and my husband seek to enlist the 27 million small business owners into a mighty political force to help "save our country" and to reverse the trends toward SOCIALISM. Please look up www.oscarpoole.com.

I am happy to share in this success story. On June 2, 2009 we celebrated 59 years of marriage. We courted two years before that! I have, therefore, known Oscar for 61 of his 79 years! Only one! The world couldn't handle two!

Oscar and Edna

Oscar & Edna Poole

Oscar, Edna, & Johnny Isakson

THERE'S ONLY ONE

Oscar & Edna Poole in Work Gear

# Endorsements

*"Oscar Poole's life is an American story — God, country, and family; struggles, defeats and victories. From the pulpit to pork, he has served and inspired all of us."*
— Jack Kingston, Congressman, First District of Georgia


*"Oscar Poole is more than a good friend. He is a friend to the world. He lives his truth as outlined in his words, deeds and personal unfoldment in a lively, entertaining and inspirational way. From political leaders, statesmen, students and the ordinary citizen, we all benefit from his presence on this planet. There is only one Oscar Poole."*
— Rev. Dr. Reginald G. Johnson, Spiritual Leader, Unity Church of the Mountains; Host of WOW Radio


*"Oscar Poole is an American classic. An American story of what hard work and liberty combined can induce. America is a great nation because it allows millions of Oscar Poole's to work, save, and succeed — LIBERTY is what happens when the government LEAVES US ALONE."*
— Grover Norquist, President, Americans for Tax Reform; Author, "Leave Us Alone"

## There's Only One

*"Oscar Poole's success story is most remarkable; he and his wife, Edna, started with no money and built a world-famous restaurant. There is no better representative of the 27 million small businesses in America than Oscar Poole, a marketing genius. He is a free enterprise champion. There is ONLY ONE Oscar Poole!"*
— Joe McCutchen, Host; "Focus on Excellence," TV talk show;
Publisher, "The McCutchen Newsletter"

*"Oscar Poole is a hardworking, respectable, salt of the earth guy. I am honored to call him my friend."*
— Saxby Chambliss, U.S. Senator

*"Oscar Poole is one of the most colorful characters I've come to know in North Georgia. He's a loyal conservative, successful, small businessman, and his pork is the kind we like in Washington. If his book is as good as his barbecue, you'll read it, enjoy it, and tell your friends about it!"*
— Nathan Deal, R-GA, Congressman, 9th District, Georgia; Candidate for Governor of Georgia, 2010

*"In over 32 years of public life, I have known many citizens who have had a lasting impact on their community, but none more than Oscar Poole. Oscar lives the American Dream every day, and he shares it with everyone he meets. Oscar's barbecue is fantastic, as is his spirit, but nothing surpasses his love of free enterprise and the opportunity that is America."*
— Johnny Isakson, U.S. Senator

## Oscar Poole

*"Barbecue Baron Oscar Poole, long a champion of God, country and free enterprise, gives us all a compelling model for success."*
   — Phil Kent, Author, Member of Georgia Gang on WAGA TV, Atlanta

*"Oscar Poole has been a dear and close friend for several years. He is a very unique being of how God will change your life. Oscar has proven how speaking will produce the results you want. He is an excellent writer, full of humor, and has a giving heart."*
   — Gary Sigler, President, Sigler Ministries

*"Colonel Poole is an icon, not only in Northwest Georgia, but throughout the state. In addition to serving some of the best barbecue around, Col. Poole is also a great patriot who promotes responsible government throughout our communities. Georgia has been greatly served by his patriotism, community service and fine barbecue!"*
   — Dr. Paul Broun, Congressman, 10th District, Georgia

*"There is no greater invention than when you learn to live your own life. That is Oscar Poole. He can scarcely contain his life's purposes. Unlike many who try to impress, Oscar doesn't turn it on and off, depending on whom he is around. He bubbles with it. He doesn't just tell you to take it easy and go with the flow, either ... he actually pulls you into his life ... and gives you a ringside seat of what it's like to live in the NOW. What a ride!"*
   — Kris Weeks, High Technology Consultant, Pennsylvania DOT

*"It is truly an honor to know Oscar Poole. Oscar has served as a mentor and friend for many of us. The entrepreneurial vision and passion for life shared by Oscar has been an inspiration that will be remembered for generations to come."*
— Kevin Harris, 9th District Republican Chair, Georgia

*"A good example, family provider, spiritual teacher, political leader and friend ... words. These are positive words that try to describe a man who listens when God talks to him and then follows instructions. God will give you new meaning for these words if you get to know my friend, Oscar Poole."*
— J.C. Sanford, Gilmer County Board of Commissioners

*"Over the years I have enjoyed Oscar's conservative views, and especially his barbecue!"*
— George N. Bunch III, Publisher, "Times-Courier"

*"From Ellijay, Georgia, to Washington, D.C., Colonel Poole has been a champion of the conservative movement and has served as an example of the values we should all strive to uphold. His entrepreneurial spirit personifies the American Dream, and his story will undoubtedly inspire America's next generation of small businessmen and women."*
— Dr. Phil Gingrey, U.S. Congressman, 11th District, Georgia

*"Col. Oscar Poole brings wisdom, strength, and a spirit to each and every person he meets. I encourage you to follow, listen and learn from this wonderful man and the example he sets. I treasure his friendship."*
— Cherie Martin, Host of *North Ga. Now Today*, ETC 3

# Chapter I
# The Life of Col. Dr. Oscar Poole

## *A modern day Entrepreneur -Statesman-Theologian-Philosopher*

### *Personal note*

This book is written about me, by me! Why? Because I know me better than anyone else! I have lived with myself for 79 years — having lived through 13 presidents, five wars, four recessions. I could have sought a more professional writer, but decided the content of my life was more important and besides, I am a little professional myself!

### Why this book?

Because my life has been so strangely beautiful — nothing short of a living romance, I decided I should do this for my posterity ... that when I am gone, I'll still be around, through my books, musical CDs and a continuing family business (a legend and landmark in Georgia). My earlier books were written to record some of my core beliefs, which, when written I knew would not be read until my passing. Especially I think this is true within my own family! (I believe this may be true in most cases, so this thought alone gives some comfort and saves me from a feeling of rejection!)

## *A spiritual journey*

My life has been a spiritual journey, that is, a journey of spirit. It has not been easy. I believe most of my experiences have been normal — although I perceive myself as nothing normal! Abnormal? Let the reader decide! Unique, at the least. I do think the reader will be amused and impressed at the variety of experiences my life poses.

This is a developing story. Change has been about the only constant. Why this? Because over the years I have developed a "theology for change!" I see clearly that change is a vital part of living, and it is something to be accepted. It has not been easy for me to grow out of the old and into the new, but it has been the most rewarding, though often challenging! I see change as a freeing experience. Yes, my life has been on the go, from the word "go," and it is still going! To where, you may ask! I am 79 years of age and it seems I am only getting started! This keeps me abreast with the changes all around me. It keeps me challenged, excited and often wondering what's next! Yes, life for me continues to be adventuresome. I find myself eager to face the next phase! Who wants to go with me?!

## *Added note*

I have chosen to write this book in the first person. That's because I am the one writing it! I have begun writing it at our home in Astor, Florida, down on the Saint John's River, one hour from New Smyrna Beach, my birthplace.

Oscar Poole Goes to Washington

There's Only One

Typical Rally

Poole's Tourist Camp

# Chapter II
# The Times of My Birth

I was born on U.S. Hwy. 1, 657 North Orange Street in New Smyrna Beach, Florida, into an old-fashioned tourist environment. The date was April 29, 1930.

They said that I was "so ugly they slapped my mother!" I don't really think this was the truth! I tell folks that I was born in a hospital, as I wanted to be near my mother. Well, this is not true either, as I was delivered in the front bedroom of our old house. The first person I ever saw on earth was a mid-wife, a black woman whom my dad paid $5. Why not a hospital? We didn't have one. And besides, my 51-year-old father would have been too tight (conservative) to pay the extra!

They called me Oscar after my father's first name. Lord only knows where they got my middle name — Cuthbert! I'm told it is a prestigious name, so I guess that's me. "Oscar" is Celtic, meaning "spear of divinity" or "fighter for God!" Well, I am divine, and I've been through so many church fights!

My dad was from South Georgia (Gibson in Glascock County, near Augusta) and my mother, a saint, was from a 40-acre family farm, near Crestview, Florida, so you see, I have real southerners for parents.

## *Tourist environment*

My parents owned and operated Poole's Camp — 24 wooden cabins, a two-story clubhouse and the "big house," two-stories, with a hand-pumped gas station and little corner grocery store.

## *Eclectic*

This old-timey tourist environment shaped my early eclecticism and appreciation for cultures other than my own southern heritage. These Yankees stayed all winter, some for 25 to 30 winters. They were Pennsylvania Dutch, from New York City (New York City?!), Boston, Canada, Ohio, Indiana — all over the north. My memory is vivid, sitting around a campfire, listening to World War I stories. It stretched my life 20 years back into American history. I can almost hear now the sounds of the drumbeat and the bombs bursting all around. What a heritage! Good old-fashioned southern parents and a cosmopolitan worldview in the making. Circa 1933-1940.

## *A funny story*

One day they couldn't find Oscar, aged three. I was lost. A neighborhood search was begun. Police! Neighbors! Panic! My mother noticed the back door of our long display ice box was open. There I was, inside the ice box, eating bananas. She said I had the whole stalk — and I was ever after "full of bananas!"

## *O.M. Poole*

That's my dad! He was born in 1879 — 14 years after the assassination of Abraham Lincoln. He was 23 years old when the Wright brothers flew their airplane. He'd be 130 years of age were he alive today.

Every time I heard the name O.M. Poole, I heard the universal sound — OM or OHM — this is from the Hindu Sanskrit, and it has given my dad cultural sophistication. A man who only attended the fourth grade, who picked 100 pounds of cotton per day on his hands and knees. A man who plowed behind mules for days on end.

## *That South Georgia food!*

Fried chicken, country ham, redeye gravy, blue ribbon cane syrup, field peas, ho-cake cornbread — you see this is my culture! Unless you have tasted South Georgia food, you don't know what you're missing! Butter beans! (I could go on.)

While I was born and reared in Florida, my South Georgia heritage looms BIG!

## *More on my dad*

My father stands out today as one of the heroes in my life. His frugality, tight-wad conservatism and his work ethic helped shape me and make me what I am today. My dad did not have an MBA (my son Greg has that!) Instead, my father had the MM (Master of Mules) degree!

I guess right here would be as good a place as any to list my dad's conservative values. These are not done in any stylish form.

## Conservative values of O.M. Poole:

- NEVER BORROW (think of the money saved on interest!)
- DO WITHOUT, DO WITHOUT, DO WITHOUT! Just do not buy it!
- FORGET THE JONES! (And all the rest of that high-falootin' crowd!)
- SHOP AT RUMMAGE SALES! I will never forget the corduroy jacket my mother bought for me for 50 cents at Mrs. Schubigger's rummage sale, on Canal Street. I was so proud of it, I wore it in August! Do you know how hot it gets in Florida in August?!
- **HEAVY WORK, WORK, WORK!** The Pooles invented it!
- Get up at 4 a.m.! We sometimes overslept until 4:30 or 5:00 a.m.!
- Pay no attention to what THEY say!
- Never give up!
- Be disciplined!
- Have GOALS! Know what you want and stay with it!

- NO CAR PAYMENTS — nor payments of any kind! My dad could not spell the word "debt," nor did he even say it!
- Buy LAND at low prices!
- When HORSE-TRADING never let on like you really wanted the thing bartered for. I've seen my father walk off from a bargain only to be called back and pay his ridiculously low price! I would even be embarrassed!
- Make a place for God in your life! When Sunday came we headed to church in the used 1934 Ford V-Eight! My dad would hook the screen door of our little "O.M. Poole Grocery" (and hand pumped filling station) with a homemade sign by my father which read, "Gone to church, be bak by noon." Yes, back was spelled 'bak'!)

I must tell about my first Hermeneutics lesson (a fancy word for Bible interpretation, learned from graduate study many years later). I can see the place in the road now! We had just turned up Wayne Avenue from Old Riverside Drive. I heard my mother discussing the day's sermon. She said, "I could not find three points in Brother Holiday's sermon today," as she analyzed what the preacher said! Of course, I was present in the service, having always sat on the second row. I didn't listen to anything the preacher said that day, as I was staring at the ceiling wondering how the electricity traveled down the chain holding the rather large light!

— Rest every afternoon in the "cool of the day!" That was around 4 p.m., but I do not remember it being cool, especially in the summertime.
— Respect others' property!

— Be friendly! I can see my dad now as he sat out by the shuffleboards with me by his side. I think I saw one picture of his arm around me, though I have not one memory of being hugged by either of my parents. I do not see this as a positive in my dad or mother, but as a weakness. Oh, these simple, hard-working, honest people may have been lacking in some matters I hold dear, but they made up for it in many other ways!

## *My own conservative values*

For those who know me I am sure they can see much resemblance in me as I have practiced many of the same virtues and values I have attributed to my father in this book. The "Col. Poole's Georgia BAR-B-Q, Inc." stands today in East Ellijay, Georgia attesting to what the reader is right now reading! In fact, even as I am writing, I find myself having joined with Joe McCutchen, one of our nation's top conservatives in forming the **"Joe McCutchen-Col. Poole Small Business Coalition,"** designed to encourage entrepreneurship throughout America in a time of one of our nation's most serious crises!

Do I ever appreciate my dad's conservative values — more so every day!

OSCAR POOLE

## *Waiting for the cotton to be unloaded*

The place was Matthews, Georgia. My dad was parked in line at the cotton gin awaiting his turn to have his cotton (picked by hand) ginned and bailed. While the mule and wagon sat there he went down to a nearby creek and caught some fresh fish and sold them for 10 to 15 cents. That little money stayed with him and when more came his way he bought farmland, a mule, or a plow.

## *Homemade ice cream and boiled peanuts*

On Saturdays my dad went to town (Uvalda, near Vidalia where the famous onions come from). Part of his first family helped him hand-crank the ice cream churn, selling a serving of ice cream for five cents. The ice for the whole occasion only cost five cents! The milk and eggs came from their little farm, three miles out in the country near where the Ocmulgee and the Oconee Rivers form the famous Altamaha River. They also sold boiled peanuts that they grew on the farm. This became their cash flow ... although it did not flow — it stayed with them because they saved it.

## *The ferry boat*

From 1920-24 my father operated a little ferry across the Altamaha River, between Uvalda and Hazelhurst. During those four years, my dad was able to save $24,000, kept in glass mason jars. That was $6,000 per year! When the bridge was finally built, the ferry business was over. But during those four years those New York Yankees who came to Florida in the falls and returned each spring spread their stories about the promised land down in Florida! Like a Tom Sawyer, my dad began to dream about moving to Florida. By now he had saved a small fortune — so off to Florida! They landed in old New Smyrna and purchased almost a city block. My father's first wife came down, took one look at all the work facing them, turned around and went back to Georgia and never returned! My dad married Sally Geanette Cain and it wasn't long until I appeared on the scene.

## *The Poole historical "claim to fame"!*

This is about Henry Pool (the "e" was added later to make us look more sophisticated!) Henry fought under General George Washington and was my great grandfather — three times over.

Well do I remember the day at age five (1935) when my father, Cluese, my half brother, and I traveled over to visit two old sisters, aged 85 and 87, daughters of Henry Pool. They were born when their father was 90 years old! These ladies were two of the last seven surviving daughters of the American Revolution (DAR) and the last two living in Georgia! They were featured in the Sunday edition of the Atlanta Journal in 1935 and I still have a copy of it!

A point I want to share is that I saw with my own eyes my distant cousins, two sisters whose father was a soldier in General George Washington's army! Of course, at the time I had no idea who they were and could have cared less! What does a little boy aged five know about things like that? I did not know this story until I was in my late 50's when some of our family researched our family history.

I know the reader might find this hard to believe, but I am a living witness to it. When the truth of this story dawned upon me, American History shrunk. Do the math: The time is 1935, the sisters age 85 and 87. They were born circa 1850, when Henry Pool was 90. Back that up to 1760 — this is before the Revolutionary War in 1776. Here it is 2009 and I'm still living! Just think I met two ladies, daughters of one of George Washington's soldiers — a direct connection with American history. And these are my kinfolks! Just goes to show how much a part of America we Pooles are! I sort of feel proud of this heritage! I really do!

## *The Baptist Sunday school*

I came running into the house one day when my mother said excitedly, "How would you like to go to Sunday school?" Keep in mind I'm only three! That sounded *big* to me!

Mrs. Ben Ard and Mrs. Williams were in our neighborhood store one day and told my mother, "If you'll get Oscar ready next Sunday, we'll pick him up and take him to Sunday school!" For four years we never missed! Perfect attendance! Little bars to prove it! In fact, this began a period of 57 ½ years in which I never missed a single Sunday!

You might wonder why the record ended. That's another story and we might get to that later!

Impressions! Wow! They taught me that **God is love**. That someone named Jesus loved me! Taught me a song about it! Jesus became a hero to me as they told me about all those wonderful deeds he performed!

I was told that Jesus "loved all the children of the world" — red and yellow, black and white — and we should, too! All of this formed the basis for much of what I believe today. Am I thankful for this part of my heritage! Especially Mrs. Ard and Mrs. Williams, two great saints in my life. They taught me well. What respect I hold in my heart for these dear hearts and gentle people — who lived and loved in my hometown!

## *My church connections*

So, from age three until seven, I attended the local First Baptist Church. When I was seven years old my father pulled me out of the Baptist Sunday school and took his family, my three sisters, Jeanette, Shirley and Wynelle, to the First Methodist Church, where I sat every Sunday on the left corner of the second pew. My mother and the rest of the family were seated right behind me on the third pew, where my sisters all wiggled. I sat still. This caught the attention of many of the ladies of the congregation as to how *well-behaved* I was! My behavior was conditioned by my fear of what would happen at home following the service, but there was no need for any of that, as reverence for God was a part of me, and after all this was the house of God. Many times I sat there wondering how the electricity flowed through the chain that held up the chandelier in the sanctuary!

## *Billy Brown*

I begin this day of writing deeply moved as I have lost one more of my dearest friends on earth, Billy Brown. I received word of Billy's passing last night. I interrupted the writing of this book for this *breaking news.* I always greeted him by singing "Where Have You Been Billy Boy." Billy came into my life in the fifth grade at the old Faulkner Street School. We students would get Billy to sing "Ole Shep" so our teacher, Miss Griffin, would cry! Billy played the guitar (taught himself) and made it to the Grand Ole Opry in Nashville! I have a picture of Billy with Gene Autry. Billy was a favorite of Autry and could have become another Elvis Presley — he was that good! But Billy "got religion" and dropped out because such things as the Grand Ole Opry were "sin." It has always grieved me at much of what this Bible-belt religion did to us. It robbed many of us of our self-esteem and stifled creativity. I believe Billy is one of those cases. I'll cover more of these views later in this book and discuss some of how and why most of my theology changed over the years of my earthly pilgrimage. Anyhow, God bless Billy Brown!

## *Georgia red clay*

I have been sharing my heritage amongst the red clay country of South Georgia. I have done this to provide a setting or context and the simple way of life that was *birthed* into me.

## There's Only One

I remember just south of Augusta, Georgia, riding in our 1928 Model A. Those hills were like mountains to me! We'd speed up the Model A to make it up the next hill. We went fast. Thirty-five or forty miles per hour! Up one hill and over the next.

In 1935 my family purchased our used 1933 Ford V-8, it was faster! We could go 50 mph!

Did I ever feel proud to ride to town with my dad. I propped my left foot under my body so I could sit up higher and look out the window! We'd ride down Riverside Drive — the back way — every Monday morning to the Sam's Gulf Oil docks to pay our bills for our hand-pumped gas station. Once I took some beans from our store and dropped them into the Indian River and called for a mermaid to come out of the water. I had seen a beautiful sexy mermaid in the Pop Eye funny papers and decided I'd like to have one. You guessed it — *no mermaid!* Oh, by the way, we sold gas for 7.9 cents per gallon. We had to pump gas into a 10-gallon glass container and it gravity flowed as we pumped gas into customer's cars. Once some kids drove their Model T into our station and bought a nickel's worth.

## *Milking cows*

I began milking two cows per day at the age of seven. Then fed the chickens. Took the cows to pasture. Sometimes we'd paint a portion of one of our wooden cabins — all before school, which began at 8:00 a.m. My dad obviously wanted to teach me some *responsibility!* By the way, these cows had to be milked again at the end of the day. I was experiencing what we now call 24/7!

## *The roar of the Atlantic Ocean*

I was awakened each day to the roar of the Atlantic Ocean as we were only two blocks from a three-mile open spaced flat land that allowed the noise of the ocean to be heard. I can hear it now. It is lodged in my memory.

## *German submarines*

One day we heard about 20 loud explosions. It was a convoy of U.S. warships attacking German submarines just off the coast of New Smyrna Beach, 15 miles south of Daytona Beach. We all ran over to the beach, and there it was! It could not have been over three miles out! A convoy of 15 or 20 tankers loaded with oil from South America headed north, and three large battleships escorting. This wasn't the only time the war came close to us. Years later Judd Dando, on patrol duty with the U.S. Coast Guard, told me that one quiet night he and his companion actually overheard German sailors talking aboard one of the German subs as they were only a few yards away. Several oil tankers were blown up and washed ashore during the war years.

I might add that my dad was both an air-raid warden and a spotter for airplanes as they passed by (I see I'm getting a little ahead of my journey, so I'll return to my pre-first grade days.)

## *Uncle Denny and Mrs. Farrell*

I can't leave them out. Every year on my birthday, beginning April 29, 1932 when I was age two, they would take me to Daytona Beach to get "Daytona Cookies" (Fig Newtons). As we approached Turnbull Bay, I was standing between Uncle Denny and Mrs. Farrell in their 1934 Ford V-8 two-door roadster. I exclaimed loudly — "See 'da wibba Unca Denny, see 'da wibba!" (U.S. Hwy. 1 was a single lane road and when meeting another car you had to pull off to the side to pass!) The Farrells were like family to me and I couldn't tell the difference! They were from Binghamton, N.Y. and spent their winters with us in Cabin Number 7. They were typical of the many Yankees (northerners) who vacationed at our tourist camp every winter. You can see how I was influenced into a cosmopolitan way of thinking by my early environment. I am truly thankful for these influences in my life. Oh the memories! How I long for those dear people — and do I ever miss them!

Having been raised among southern people it was hard for me to hate Yankees! There was still that old consciousness hanging around from the Civil War. Especially could I not hate those who supported us financially! That thought never entered my head. It was the other — LOVE! It came naturally, long before I even heard of a Civil War! As I have grown older I have come to believe that hate, meanness-of-spirit, and the like, are "learned" and not passed on by genes or DNA. You may be guessing it. I do not believe in the foolish doctrine of

## O8CAR POOLE

*original sin!* I did not come here a sinner and I never saw a toddler rob a bank!

# A vision at age 5!

When I was five years of age I kept having an impressive vision. I dreamed there was out in front of me an *ocean of faces.* They could not be numbered. As far as my eye could see — they faded into infinity! This happened many times, so many it was indelibly impressed into my subconscious! It appears before me even as I write these words. Its' meaning? Certainly it was a great coming together! As I have pondered this seemingly real experience I have wondered if it is *prophetic!* It's been there for 74 years! Maybe someone reading this has had a similar vision!

# Another word about Billy Brown

Billy's funeral was held last night at a church in nearby New Smyrna Beach, one hour from here. Of course it was sad. Somewhat comforting as the people did the best they could. There were huge amounts of love poured out on my dear friend Billy. But I witnessed what I feel is a *great tragedy.* The pastor, reflecting his fundamentalist views, seemed proud that Billy was offered an opportunity to join Gene Autry and Ernest Tubb. But he lauded Billy's turning down the offer of stardom and compared Billy to Moses' renouncing the *pleasures of sin* for a season to suffer with the people of God! So Billy turned the "bad" thing down, playing and singing for the Grand Ole Opry, when he could have blessed millions! Here is a prime example of religion getting in the way of one achieving his life's dream. It was in my opinion, a betrayal of not only what already was, but what was well on the way of *becoming!* Rather than destroy the potential in people I want to *affirm* it! I see what the world missed by not enjoying the blessings of a fully developed Billy Brown! This is one of my gripes about organized religion — amongst many. I believe Jesus came to save us *from* religion — not in it! Here I've gone to preaching (pontificating) and I ask the reader to forgive me! I just couldn't help it! This is exactly how I feel. You had to have heard Billy Brown! He was one of a very few! (You can see some of my theology as seen through my eyes at age 79 — a "progressive" journey of faith.)

## *Sally Geanette Cain Poole*

That's my sainted mother! What a vital part of my life! Throughout this book she will play a major role.

My mother was 21 years younger than my dad and loved him dearly. Her love for her children was no less! Oftentimes she would intercede for me and my father when she felt he was going a little too far in his discipline of me!

Sally Poole was born in Baker, Fla., over in the extreme panhandle of the state — right next to the Alabama line. She was raised by John and Beulah Cain on a 40-acre farm that I am sure was land-granted to their ancestors. I've been there several times. They had no screens on the windows, only wooden shutters. The little house was high off the ground with cracks in the floors. They had no car. On Saturdays my

## OSCAR POOLE

grandfather walked to town, Crestview, a distance of seven miles, to purchase flour and other food staples. My mother told me he spent 10 to 15 cents for candy for the children — one cent for each child. They chewed pine rosin for chewing gum! They did have a mule, a plow and several cows. The whole family worked, plowing behind the mule and chopping cotton.

They were poor, but proud! They went to school only as far as the eighth grade, as there were no high schools in the area. No school buses, they walked! That part of Northwest Florida was also *red clay* country. All the roads were clay except one paved highway which wandered around curves with steep banks.

Once I remember we all went down to an old fashioned swimming hole! It was not a nicely manicured pond like you see scattered throughout the countryside today, just a wide spot in a meandering stream wandering through the woods! Nearly all of us had some kind of clothes on except some of us children! It didn't really matter about us.

My mother's youngest brother, Levy, survived the attack on Pearl Harbor as he had enlisted in the U.S. Navy. No one knew he had survived until nearly a month later as communication was almost *nil* in those days — no television (didn't even know about it), no cell phones, only a few newspapers and Atwater-Kent radios! My Uncle Levy became a World War II hero and remained so in Titusville, Florida, where he was a grand marshal in all the parades until his passing about five or six years ago. Levy went to Florida State University on the G.I.

Bill, and was my mother ever proud of him! A college graduate in our family!

My mother dressed her four children nicely! I saw a picture at my sister, Wynelle Smith's house only last night. There we sat, all four of us, I in my little sailor suit with Jeannette (we called her "Sister"), Shirley, and I holding "Baby," Wynelle, my youngest sibling. We were cute! The way we were dressed revealed the pride she had in her children! I must say I was a bit surprised at the "uptown-ness" of our appearance as my mother often made my father's shirts out of feed sacks! No feed sacks here! It was some bind of finery — must have been Easter or something like that!

## *Preachers were my heroes*

During those tender years, from age three until seven, it was only natural that preachers should become my heroes! These men spoke FOR God! Wow! How higher could one get than that? They were BIGGER-THAN-LIFE! When my dad invited the preacher home for Sunday dinner, I would be so proud — and of course, on excellent behavior. What a treat! Let's don't forget that my father was on his *best behavior* also. I'm saying this because my father had a bad habit of criticizing my mother and finding fault with the rest of us. He was much older (51 when I was born and had three more children after that!). He must have gotten his *grouchy attitude* from some of that strict upbringing back in South Georgia. These pastors were on their best behavior, too! We all were.

## Oscar Poole

I will never forget the meal we were having when I casually spoke up and told my father what Miss Griffin (my fifth grade teacher), said about eating food and digesting it. She said when eating your food that there should be no harsh words, arguing, or finding fault, lest you could not digest your food properly! When I said this it seemed my father received a little correction from a little child — me, his son — while my mother "had a ball!" I laughed out loud! It was one of those *rare moments* where it seemed I was in total control. And, I hardly even tried.

## *Once we had an accident*

On Hwy. 1 near Jacksonville, we were returning from Uvalda, Ga., loaded with freshly butchered hogs (maybe this was a precursor to my "taking Pork back to Washington" events, chickens and all!). Anyhow we were driven off the road and into the ditch. Fortunately we were not driving fast as 35-40 mph was about as fast as the car would go. We weren't hurt except for a scar I still carry over my left eye. They said chickens flew everywhere — a sight to behold! But I do not remember this as I was probably only two.

## *Summary*

There you have it — the "times" into which I was born. The early part of the 20th century: the era of Ford Tri-motor airplanes, the Atwater-Kent radios, plenty of Ford Model A's, church every Sunday — hardly any place else to go, gasoline 7.9 cents a gallon, hearses for ambulances, going to elementary school barefooted. I remember well each evening listening to "Amos & Andy" radio shows and "Lum & Abner" and hearing Lum answering the phone, "Jottem Down Store, Lum speaking!"

I have spoken highly of my South Georgia roots. Those conservative, hard-working farm values have made me what I am today and I am proud of this heritage! I think the old fashioned southern way of life along with the "Yankees" on my dad's tourist camp, and my family, are the most influential in the formation of who I am! I am truly thankful for both my southern heritage and the strong northern influence.

# Chapter III
# Grammar School

At age six, I went to school at the old Faulker Street School, where I spent the next six years studying "reading, writing and arithmetic, danced to the tune of a hickory stick!" But in this case it was Miss Patillo's wooden paddle! I can still feel the heat on my bottom! I know what being sent to the principal's office meant. I only received two paddlings the whole six years — one from Miss Patillo, and the other from Miss Griffin, in the fifth grade. Add to that the other two paddlings I got when I went home!

Of course, the only means of transportation was walking. How well do I remember stubbing my toe on a tree root that protruded up through the sidewalk!

## *The alphabet*

One day I stood by the blackboard and asked Miss Hastings, my first grade teacher, what that long word was at the top of the blackboard that started *way over here* and went *way over there!* "What is that word?" I asked. She replied (I can hear it now), "That's not a word, that's the alphabet!" "Does it spell 'alphabet'?" I asked. "It doesn't spell anything!" So I concluded by saying, "Well, if it doesn't spell anything, I'm not going to learn it!" Why learn all those letters if it didn't spell anything!

I do remember the first word I learned: "A." That wasn't too difficult. Other words followed: "cat," "at," "dog" — then later those "big" words like "house" and "school". So, in my childlike stubbornness I did not commit to learning the alphabet until one day during recess in the fourth grade. It *dawned* on me that if I learned the alphabet I could do all the words! I had it down pat (colloquialism) in ten minutes.

From grades two through six, I had the responsibilities of milking the two cows, feeding the chickens, as well as other chores, all before walking the one-half mile to school.

I need to mention that it was during the first grade that Elwood Howard came into my life. He's still there and lives in Ft. Collins, Colorado at the writing of this book. Elwood had an electric train and I went to his home often to play with it. I thought such people were *rich* and that we were too poor. Little did I realize that we were not poor, but my dad was too stingy! We could afford such things probably more than anyone else in town. I just didn't know it. I remember in the second grade my mouth watering for one of those orange popsicles, but I never did get one. Instead, I waited until I got home when we had plenty of homemade buttermilk! I ought to know — I churned it! I think everybody needs an electric train and I believe my dad's lack of appreciation was a weakness on his part, but I understand now where he was coming from.

## The advent of Billy Brown

Billy showed up in Miss Griffin's class when we were in the fifth grade. His family moved to New Smyrna Beach from Princeton, West Virginia. His father worked for the F.E.C. Railroad. Billy loved country music, especially the guitar. So at age ten he bought one himself, with money earned by selling some kind of salve I had never heard of! He taught himself to play the guitar and would go down to Canal Street and play and sing his little country tunes! His most famous song was "Ole Shep,' which he sang many times just to make Miss Griffin Cry! We loved the crying more than the music!

## Don't forget Breece McCray

All during grades one through six, Breece McCray was one of my closest friends and colleagues. We were in Sunbeams (a children's class in the local Baptist church) together. Breece could not pronounce "Oscar", so he called me "Ockee!" He still does! Breece later became the youngest mayor in the whole state of Florida, of our hometown, New Smyrna Beach.

## Next to the moon!

All during my early days I thought we lived at the end of the world! I had no idea we were next door to where the first man would travel to the moon — Cape Canaveral (known as Cape Kennedy from 1963 to 1973). Some things are so obvious you overlook them. Here we were — in a paradise! A small town where you could walk under the glare of streetlights, pick oranges out of your backyard, play in the streets, and live the *American Dream.* Somebody should have told me that then! Maybe they did and like Edna says often, "You did not listen!"

## *My piano debut*

In the fourth grade, or earlier, I developed an interest in the piano. I loved to hear the great pianists play the classics — Beethoven, Chopin, and others.

I asked my parents repeatedly if I could take piano lessons. Finally they gave in. So off to Mrs. Kicklighter's house I went! I rushed home to announce, "Look Mom, I can play the piano with both hands! And, I could — after one lesson — play the song, "Indians, Indians, Everywhere" — just three notes. Thus began my piano pilgrimage.

My first piano performance was in church. In an old-fashioned tent revival in November of 1939, one of the coldest winters I can remember — we warmed ourselves by charcoal pots. It was Elizabeth Venum who asked if I'd play the offertory. Was I ever excited! I chose a very small two-line hymn and did I practice! Fourth grade. Piano solo. In church. Wow! I drew straight lines from the top notes to the bottom ones so I could play them together! Out of a little paperback book — my first performance in public!

Often Mr. Schubigger, our high school principal, would have me play in our assemblies. When they clapped it felt good! Of course, this was a few years later, but it all began in the fourth grade!

## *Helen Keller*

It's almost hard to believe that I actually met Helen Keller! About the third grade they brought the famous Helen Keller to our church, then the old First Methodist Church. They turned out the lights! It was pitch dark! You could not see your hand in front of your face. She played the piano in the dark. Of course, she was blind, but what beautiful music came through her spirit and her hands! I think this experience may have played a big part in my own inspiration to play the piano!

## *The bombing of Pearl Harbor*

I am now age 11. I have just walked home from church, it is Sunday evening and my dad is *glued* to the radio and the voice of Edward R. Murrow. "THE JAPANESE HAVE JUST BOMBED PEARL HARBOR!" My dad's mood was that we are not prepared! He seemed very worried! The next day our teacher, Mrs. Miller, had us listen to President Franklin D. Roosevelt (FDR) as he addressed the joint session of the U.S. Congress. I remember FDR calling this a DASTARDLY (he elongated the middle syllable "tard") attack and called it a "day that will live in infamy!" His voice cracked on the word "infamy." I heard it for the first time, within minutes we were at war. World War II had begun.

# There's Only One

The very next day we went into gas rationing. The "gas" part didn't really matter to us as we parked the car — except for maybe one trip per week to church and back on Sunday. Walking and riding our bicycles. That went on for the *duration,* as we called it. That was until May of 1945 when the war ended. One month before that, FDR died. I remember well having "extras" — added editions of the newspaper — opportunity to earn a little extra money. Harry S. Truman became our president! I would meet with him, *privately*, a few years later!

Oscar's Model T

# Chapter IV
# Junior High

The year is 1942. The war is raging. Shots are heard off our shores — the German submarines alluded to earlier! Victory gardens! I think we did our part, as it seemed we must have had twenty or thirty of them! Work! Work! Work!

## *My first paying job*

I had a paper route with the Miami Herald. Graham Howie stopped by our corner store, the O.M. Poole Grocery — and offered me my first paper route — South End, Edgewater, and North End — a total distance of SEVEN miles! Imagine pedaling a bicycle for seven miles, all before breakfast. Don't forget school! Out of bed at 4 a.m. for the responsibility of meeting old train number 76 at 4:20, already one mile pedaled to get to the train station!

I remember my first salary! It was on a Saturday, the day I pedaled the whole route twice! Once for the morning delivery and another time during the day. Fourteen miles! Can you believe this? Twelve years old, seventh grade, fourteen miles! Even now it stretches my imagination to believe this. I did this for about three years, until the route expanded and I bought my first car — a cut-down 1936 Ford, which we called a "Skeeter!" That came during the tenth grade.

It was time to receive my first week's wages. I brought the money I had collected to Mr. Graham's house where he "piled it up" on top of a big table. I will never forget the amazing sight! He counted out seven one-dollar bills. "That," Mr. Howie said, "is yours!" Wow, seven dollars — one dollar for each seven-mile day. Big money! My eyes must have bulged. That seven dollars grew to *fifty* per week later in high school, and I'll have more to say about that as the book progresses.

## *Church pianist*

I became the church pianist in 1942 at the age of twelve, lasting for ten years through college. They tell me I got pretty good *fast!* After a little over two years of piano lessons I'm playing for people to sing! Sundays at 11 a.m., 7:30 p.m., and Wednesday night prayer service. You can see that I was receiving great discipline in these formative years! But I loved it!

All during these years I listened to Rudy Atwood playing the piano for "The Old Fashioned Revival Hour" over ABC radio from Long Beach, California. Rudy became my spiritual hero and my piano mentor. Up and down. All over the piano! His spirit and mine connected. I could feel what he felt! It was nothing short of glorious! His style infiltrated mine and people said we sounded alike. This thrilled me! If you never heard Rudy Atwood play, you missed out! It was the classics incorporated into the hymns. At precisely 4 p.m. each Sunday, one second past the hour, "We have heard the joyful sound! Jesus saves! Jesus saves!" I came alive! My skin tingled! My soul resonated! I was *in tune*.

One Sunday I borrowed my pastor's webcor wire recorder and recorded the program's theme of heavenly sunshine, slowed it down and memorized it. I can play it to this day! Music has played a major role in my life. Recently I wrote my sixth little book, *"I Hear Music — What Do You Hear?"* It has become my belief that music is the language of the universe and I feel attuned to it! This does something deep on the inside of me that I cannot explain!

## *Victor Grey and O.H. Ferdon*

I said at the beginning of this book that "preachers were my heroes" because they spoke FOR God! Two of these preachers were Victor Grey from Chattanooga, Tennessee, and Ormond Hamilton Ferdon from St. Petersburg, Florida. The former, Victory Grey, stepped into my life, and interceded for me in a family matter that actually helped spare my life from a serious trauma! Bless Victor Grey!

Then came O.H. Ferdon. We had a camaraderie friendship that few ever have! A humorous incident occurred one Sunday evening when I went to sleep between verses of an invitational hymn (I was church pianist) and he told Mary Jane, a great friend, "Wake him up!" Of course, this broke any *spirit* of *conviction* that may have been operative as we all broke out into a laugh! But not me, I was embarrassed! I think she should have replied, "You wake him up! You put him to sleep!" I'm just kidding — it was the getting up at 4 a.m. every morning as I dozed off to sleep whenever I got still.

Once, on a Sunday morning I dozed off and jumped right up standing in the middle of a sermon — loud bang! Can you imagine how I felt standing there —*alone*, wondering why I'm the only one standing?

## My first views of solar energy

In the fourth grade, my colleague, Elwood Howard and I were out on the playground with paper and a small magnifying glass. We burned each other on the arm and actually started a few small fires. We never got caught! World War II was going very strong at the time and I raised the question, "Why doesn't Hitler put a large magnifying glass behind an airplane and burn up the earth?" Why I did not think of the Allies doing this I don't know! Now that we are searching for new ways to harness solar energy, I find myself asking the same question. Apparently, this solar principle is already in use in "solar panel" farms. I recently viewed one of these 100-acre farms near Wachula, Florida — a facility underway by the Florida Power & Light Corporation.

## My camp meeting days

I attended the old Suwanee River Nazarene Campground near White Springs, Florida, each year from 1940 until 1948. It was almost heaven to me! I loved everything about it! For one thing, it gave me an opportunity to get away from an overly critical father. I already mentioned that my dad was not perfect! I still hear those old camp meeting melodies floating through the air! I loved the people, and they loved me. Philip and Andy Benson became close friends. They were from the famous Benson family from Princeton, Florida, south of Miami. Rich heritage! Associating with great people creates lasting influences. Oftentimes while they were preaching in high-pitched southern rhetoric, I'd be back in the wooden benches in the sawdust floors talking with God! It was there that I experienced some profound dialogues with God — the Highest Power of the universe! I can feel myself being shaped and formed, all over again, as I write these words. It's more than just a pleasant memory — it's real!

It was one summer that I nearly drowned. We boys went down to a swimming hole in Swift Creek where I drifted out a little too far into the middle. The stream moved swiftly, I lost control of my dog paddling and I panicked! I remember my thoughts as a boy from West Palm Beach jumped in and saved me. That's a lasting experience for the memory bank. I never knew the boy's name. *Thank You* is all I can say!

The junior high years were pretty much uneventful except for my disciplines of hard work, milking the cow, delivering papers seven miles per day, practicing the piano and studying in between. There was stress, but I managed to cope with it.

When the ninth grade arrived I seemed to settle down and take studying more seriously. I remember I took five credits of study and raised my grade level from a C to a B average. No girlfriends. Did I want one? Of course, but I didn't have time!

THERE'S ONLY ONE

The Taj Ma Hog

Oscar Active in Politics
"All Politics is Local"

# Chapter V
# High School

I arrived at high school in the tenth grade. Fifteen years of age! Mr. Howie made a special deal that he would furnish $15 per week if I would purchase a car and take on some added responsibility. I jumped at the opportunity.

## *My first car*

I borrowed $150 from my father and entered into private business as an assistant agent for the Miami Herald. Big time! I had not realized it but I had been an entrepreneur on a smaller scale for the three previous years, from age 12 to 15. Apparently I had proven myself with that work ethic I discussed earlier. I had successfully met old Train 76 every day at 4:20 a.m.

What a change — now a car to deliver the seven-mile route. Thirty-five dollars per week! Unheard of! This business enterprise lasted the next five years, all through my bachelor's degree at Stetson University in nearby DeLand, Florida. I was the wealthiest student in our high school, but I did not think about this during those years. Popular? Why of course, everyone wanted to ride on my '36 Ford Skeeter! Let me describe my car — well, let's call if "half" a car, as there was no top! Someone had cut the top off with an ax — left the hood, windshield, all four fenders and both bumpers intact. The back seat was a homemade wooden bench. Seatbelts?

Who ever heard of those? No turn signals. Only signals by hand.

Each summer I drove my Skeeter to the White Springs Camp to renew my Nazarene friendships! They meant the world to me. For eight years they served as my support system.

## T.C. Wilder arrives!

Actually he appeared in the seventh grade. We'd sit outside on the park bench and eat our lunches with Walter Bennett, who lived on the beachside. C. Winston Smith, Jr. would meet with us. (Winston became a professor at Ohio University.) Then the bell rang and we went back to classes for the next three hours. It is surprising to me that none of us had girlfriends! I liked all my classmates, but I was not *attracted* to anyone. I had plenty of desire, I guess, but I know the "right one" had not appeared.

T.C. worked every afternoon at the Settle Funeral Home. Often I came by and visited with him on the way home from school. (T.C. asked me not to tell about Elwood, he and me stealing those oranges. So, I wont!)

T.C. later bought into the funeral business and the firm became known at the Settle-Wilder Funeral Home. Over fifty years later the name is the same. T.C. Wilder keeps track of our remaining classmates and gets us together three or four times per year.

OSCAR POOLE

## *Don't forget Harold Tumblin and Charles Mueller!*

When you saw one (myself included), you saw the other two. Three close friends, throughout junior and senior high. We all three had paper routes and spent many hours together. Harold had a girlfriend, Margaret. I would drive Harold's car while they sat in the backseat and smooched. Of course, they went by their "Sunday school" rules! (I couldn't really tell, as it was dark!)

All during these high school years I was prospering financially. I always had money in my pocket.

I remained church pianist all during this time, took lessons, and improved as we progressed. I played often for high school assemblies.

## *Football!*

I joined the team in the eleventh grade and played left tackle. I really did not care much about it except that I was "big" and big guys played football. I have a scar on my chin where a player from Mainland High School kicked me in the face as he came across my part of the line. None of us were standouts and we didn't win any games! But we had fun and the special *collegiality* with the players remains. I guess I ought to mention that I slipped off from my parents' knowing about my football experiences until word got back to them that I was on the team and looking pretty good! I saw them on several occasions looking through the fence on the end of the field to avoid buying a ticket! That conservatism expressed itself throughout my dad's life in many ways and places. I really think he should have been on the front row cheering for his son!

## Senior year finally arrives!

It is the fall of 1947. I am seventeen and my last year of high school commences. In the eleventh grade I had been chosen vice president of the student body, and I was chosen to attend the Southeastern Division of Student Government in secondary schools as a delegate! Four of us, two boys and two girls, spent two weeks traveling in a 1937 two-door Chevrolet. We were gone over two weekends and each Sunday my friends stopped at a church for me to attend Sunday school, as by that time I had reached 15 years of perfect attendance! That was an exciting adventure. I gained a little political experience, as this was a political convention! Preparing me for conventions to come? I sort of think so!

## My dance orchestra experience

My piano playing seems to be improving — at least Jack Birch thought so. He chose me to join his band, "Jack Birch and His Rhythm Berries." We played for local events and got invited to play at the local yacht club for dances on Saturday nights. Did I ever enjoy this! I am almost eighteen when word got out to our pastor, whose name I'll not mention because of some dear friends who remain connected to him — especially do I refer to Joyce Tumblin — another lifetime friend with whom I have always had a loving respect.

It was early one Sunday morning after we had arrived at church. The pastor approached me and said, "Oscar, you cannot play the piano today! Nor can you play again until you leave that dance band!" I was devastated! He added, "You know we cannot tolerate what you are doing! That's sin ... and you know it." Know it or not I thought my life was coming to an end. Rejected, I thought was despised! By my pastor! For three or four days I wallowed in the valley of despond. Lonely! Nowhere to go, except to Jack Birch's house and tell him I could not play in the band again. He received my resignation with sorrow. I went immediately to the pastor's house where I announced the news and confessed to my sin. This was accepted and by the next Sunday I was playing again in church.

## *The Nazarenes*

Came to town, pitched a tent on the corner of Downing and South Orange Streets, and conducted services nightly for about seven weeks. This was when I played my first piano solo mentioned earlier.

My mother "hit the sawdust trail" and became a charter member of the newly formed congregation of the First Church of the Nazarene. Seventy years later the church continues as the strongest Nazarene church in our part of the state.

So I moved from Baptist to Methodist to Nazarene! No wonder I have been an *eclectic* for most of my life! The Nazarenes brought something into our lives the others seemed to lack — a freer style of worship with testimonies, spirited singing, and even sometimes shouting! These were my teenage formative years and I am grateful for these influences in my life. These were the camp meeting days I spoke about.

The distinctive doctrine of the Nazarenes was "Second Blessing Holiness" or entire sanctification as a "second definite work of grace!" They were Armenian (that means you could "fall from grace." And did I ever practice this! I got "saved" so many times I lost count!

The "first work of grace" was when one went to the altar the first time. Then sometime later you had to go back to the altar to get sanctified. This means the old sin principal (the carnal nature) was eradicated! I mean, *gone!* The only problem was I never met one who experienced this! It seemed to me the more sanctified one got the meaner in spirit he became. This I could not accept and led me eventually to break with these people.

Being Armenian (followers of Jacobus Armenius) as opposed to the Calvinists (followers of John Calvin), who believed in that *sinful doctrine* of eternal security — once saved, always saved. Did I ever receive an indoctrination of this part of church history — even before college and seminary days! The Nazarenes were an "off-shoot" of Methodists and claimed John Wesley as their progenitor. Therefore, they called themselves Wesleyan! The Baptists, with whom I began my first four years of spiritual journey, were the *bad guys* — sinners — they practiced committing sin while we were sanctified — even sinless! Today I consider all this as moral confusion, a detriment to living the Christian life. Can you imagine the inward conflicts of a teenager growing up and having to listen to such foolishness Sunday after Sunday? (I guess my habit of sleeping in church was not so bad after all.)

## *Tension*

There was tension at every turn and I would not call it *creative*, but destructive! This was the irony of it all. While I loved the people and had many loving associations through these years, there was always that inner conflict between the desires of the flesh and the Holy — whatever that was! Oh, to be holy! And when you got there, it was boring, not very pleasant! Judging, finding fault — always putting down others whose lives exemplified even a higher standard than ours! This created a lot of confusion within me that took many years to dissipate. Sometimes I am surprised I didn't turn out to be schizophrenic! Looking back, I often felt that many of my colleagues (the Holiness people) called the good things *bad* and the bad things *good!* The scripture says "woe" to them who do that! I think I can testify to many woes along this line. Especially did this cause inner conflict in regard to those teenage feelings toward the opposite sex that are only natural during one's physical development. I never once heard that this was only normal and God-given! I had lots of feelings toward girls, but since I didn't have the time for them this was not the problem it might have been. But living near the world's safest bathing beach did cause some problems — it was a sin to even look — and I did a lot of looking. The reader is left to wonder about all that I am leaving out.

## Time to get serious about college

In the fall of 1947 I started saving $100 per month for college. The only place to go was Trevecca Nazarene College in Nashville, Tennessee, where all my spiritual friends attended. I thought of Trevecca as sort of an extension of the Nazarene Camp Meeting. The "call to preach" came as an outgrowth I think, of my early admiration of preachers as my heroes. This was my perceived spiritual mandate and this, along with the holiness emphasis of being against about everything that moved, kept me in a fairly celibate life. That might be one advantage from a negative church emphasis, but I'm not sure. After nine months I saved $900. That was $25 per week, half of my income. This was enough to pay for my first year's expenses — room, board and tuition.

## The summer of 1947

I need to mention that I did have one steady girlfriend — at a distance. I met Sherry at camp meeting. She was in the crowd and when everyone else "paired off," there we were! You can't really call it "going together" because we didn't go anywhere! We were together for only ten days at the Camp, although I did go to see her at her home in St. Petersburg. I drove my '36 Ford Skeeter across the state and she seemed to enjoy riding in it. I was never in love with Sherry, although I found out later she was with me. When we were alone together I had "too much religion" to enjoy the experience! Seriously! Knowing myself now this seems very strange to me. I don't have nearly as much religion now.

## *One date in high school*

I did ask one girl, who lived on a yacht on my paper route, for a date. I took her in my Skeeter to the picture show — the only movie theater in town, where I finally held her hand — and I am sure she could feel each heartbeat as I could feel it myself! Embarrassed, I finally pulled my hand away. After a few minutes she pushed my shoulder and said, "You're asleep!"

## *Mary Jane Snodgrass*

Mary Jane was about three years older than I. She was my closest friend outside Harold and Charles. While she was my friend, she was not a "girlfriend" — we enjoyed hundreds of hours together talking about our teenage loves. I had a crush on Diane Crawford over in High Springs, while Mary Jane actually had an active relationship with Diane's brother, Don, who was away attending Bethany Nazarene College in Oklahoma. Although I was serious about Diane, she never responded in any meaningful way toward me. Mary Jane rode in my Skeeter to the Nazarene campground each summer where we met Diane and Don. Mary Jane's relationship never materialized with Don, and mine with Diana never got off the ground!

But we'd talk — under the streetlights over on the beach side after church on Wednesday nights. Never once being romantic, we simply enjoyed being together. You see, we were both "saved" and "sanctified!" At least, Mary Jane and I never seemed to have any romantic notions toward each other. She and I were the best of friends and remained so right up until her passing a couple of years ago. I participated in her funeral service by cell phone, 500 miles away.

## *Summary*

I graduated from high school on June 4, 1948. Three weeks earlier President Harry S. Truman proclaimed Israel as a state! That began a whole new era in Mid-East politics.

I was eighteen. Hard work, strict discipline, rising at 4 a.m. seven days a week, the paper route, study, piano practice. Three months later my life would experience a drastic change, as I prepared to leave home and go off to college in Nashville — home of the Grand Ole Opry!

## Chapter VI
## My College, University Years

It is September 1948. Andy Benson has traveled from Princeton, where he joined me in riding on my Skeeter, all night Saturday and into Sunday (we picked up Louie Johnson at the Daytona Beach bus station on the way out of town).

What a sight! Three of us in an open-air car with no roof and plenty of air! About 4 a.m. we drove through old Atlanta, Georgia, on Highway 41 where a carload of "rowdy boys" chased us clear into Marietta!

We stopped at the First Church of the Nazarene in Chattanooga so I could attend Sunday school and keep my record — of 16 years! After our brief stop at the church we journeyed northward toward Nashville, over Monteagle Mountain. I shall never forget the sight as I looked back over my right shoulder at the mountain we had just crossed. I had never seen a mountain! Pain — severe pain — hit me! "What have I done?!" I asked myself. I was only 600 miles from home, but I could have been in the Yukon Territory! It really came clear to me that I was not *at home!* I was stunned for a few minutes but the pain lessened and within two hours we arrived on top of the Trevecca Campus — overlooking Nashville.

It would be safe to say I was somewhat dazed and in shock — not knowing that the *greatest shock* of my life awaited me the next day. Here we were "on a hill far away!" And did I ever feel it. During those moments, I wanted to be back in New Smyrna Beach, home where I belonged! Or at least I thought I did! I was in immediate trauma. Concurrent with all the excitement and romance of those few days, my dad was back home throwing a fit! He thought he had lost his son — me, the one he had placed all his hopes in of becoming a lawyer and a politician! To say he was *throwing a fit* is putting it mildly. He gave my mother *hell!* The anguish she was going through added much pressure on me. I was not so sure I was doing the right thing. I questioned the *rightness* of my decision and it would not have surprised me had I got back onto (not into) the car and returned. But I had acted in faith — and faith won! Those were extremely difficult moments, sorting out my feelings and emotions. For a time I bore these alone. I do not wish them upon anyone! My father actually said to me the day before we left Florida, "If you go off to college in Nashville you are no longer my son — don't come back!" How's that for a send off? But the call upon me was greater, and off to Nashville I went.

## Here comes the shock of my life

Edna, that is! Edna Yvonne Shock, from Charleston, West Virginia.

Are things about to change! Wow! And wow again!

Three girls approached me and asked if I would go to the train station and pick up a trunk for one of them — Edna. I obliged. Three of us sat in the front seat, with this West Virginia girl in the middle. No seat belts — we had to sit close. There were many *curves* between Trevecca and the train depot, so we had to *turn curves with curves* in the front seat — if you know what I mean!

That was a Monday. We started going together on Wednesday, and got married on Friday! Well, it was Friday nearly two years later! All week long we attended the fall college revival together. We sat together and held hands under the pews, even while they prayed. No sleeping this time!

The romance of the century was about to begin. It continues into the next century — 59 years when this book is published!

Life is moving fast! The pain and initial shock of arriving in Nashville is lessening. Meanwhile I got a job in West Nashville at a wire factory earning $22 per week. (Remember my income back home on my paper route was $50 per week.) I worked the 3 to 11 p.m. shift each day. As we slipped my Skeeter back onto the hill at 11:30 p.m. there was Edna looking out the window of her room — second floor of the girl's dormitory! One night I picked up my mail in the administration building and in a daily letter from Edna it read, "I think I love you!" Well, I did her. You can guess the content of our conversations for the next days and weeks. Edna even commenced talk of how she wanted her wedding! I got the feeling she was talking about me! Yes, the love story of the ages was underway. We started going together and going, and going, and going. Pretty good, wouldn't you say, for it having been said by a certain mother-in-law, "They'll never make it!"

## *Homesick for two weeks*

Edna was now the "love of my life" but this did not keep me from two weeks of extreme homesickness. After arriving back to my room in which there were six boys (three double bunks), I'd go into our private bathroom while the others were asleep and cry! Broken! My emotions were getting the best of me. I hurt. I cried more. I went on for two full weeks, then as suddenly as it came, it left! Never returned. Believe you me, homesickness is painful!

## *The "A" in Greek*

I went to class each day at 8 a.m. The first hour was New Testament Greek — surprise! I found myself at home with it. There was a lot of rote learning, memorization, and I was good at it! After twelve weeks we were taking the fall quarter's exams and would you believe I made an "A" for the quarter's work! This had a tremendous positive effect upon me! I discovered that not only could I do college work — I was good at it!

## *A college music professor at age 18!*

Something else that enhanced my self-esteem was when one day while I was taking my piano lesson, the teacher said, "We cannot teach you! We need to have you help us!" You can see that I am beginning to have a series of *shocks* happening to me. In love with a beautiful girlfriend, the "A" in Greek and now asked to "join the staff!" For the next three months I taught beginning piano students and was paid a small stipend for my efforts. Things are happening fast! All of my dating was done on weekends.

About the middle of the fall of 1948 someone came to me at work and offered to place a 1935 Ford body on my '36 Ford Skeeter. I took the offer and soon had a full car! But I couldn't afford a new battery, so I parked the car on a hill — let go of the brake, put it in gear and cranked it as it rolled down the embankment! No anti-freeze either! I kept it drained between weekends and on occasion it was too cold to crank the motor without the anti-freeze.

## *My first snow!*

Once it snowed five inches! Several of us got sleds and rode down the hill! I had never seen the first flake of snow. Eighteen years of age and having a ball — snowballs that is! We even made some snow cream. Imagine, free ice cream in a snowstorm!

## *Time for the Christmas holidays*

And, to go home! But did I have a home to go to? The words of my father began to ring louder in my ears. Edna had returned by bus to her home in West Virginia, and four of us boys headed south in my 1935-36 Ford! My passengers got off at various places and the car headed south on U.S. 1. Almost

THERE'S ONLY ONE

another traumatic moment ... I'm two blocks north of the old home place, Poole's Camp! What will I find when I arrive? Will my father receive me or tell me to keep on going? Where would I go? My heart pounded!

I drove into the front yard next to the old clubhouse. There stood my mother and of course, she welcomed me! Soon, my father came from out back. He did not throw anything at me, nor did he say many words.

I spoke prophetically to my mother! I said, " I liked college, made an "A" in Greek and I want to get a doctor's degree!" Her heart sank! She thought I meant becoming a medical doctor. "You mean," she asked, "You're not going to be a preacher?" I explained to her, "There are different kinds of doctor's degrees: some in history, some theology, some science" — little did I know that this would become true — not in the seven year span, which seemed an eternity, but many years down the road.

The two week vacation passed. Nothing was said about my not being my father's son. We made cane syrup, delivered papers (my father and my sisters had kept up the paper route), gathered oranges and a few pecans — and I headed back to Nashville!

It was the last few days of 1948! I was still in NSB (New Smyrna Beach) when the clock struck twelve the night of December 31. I left sometime up in the day, January 1, 1949. I'm on my way via Uvalda, Georgia, where I spent the night with my half-brother, Cluese. The next day, January 2, after eating some

## Oscar Poole

tender fried chicken from a chicken caught in the yard, and some biscuits cooked in a wood stove (with just the right amount of brown around the edges), I headed north again!

Past the old Talmadge Farm in McCrae, past Wesleyan College in Macon, on through Atlanta, making some good time until a little north of Ringgold, Georgia, where I got stopped by the police.

It was late in the evening. I was bouncing all over the road. Trying to keep up with the car ahead of me! The motor had to be *revved* up fast enough for the generator to put out enough light, as the battery was still low!

I saw this car trying to go around me. I listened more intently. I'd back off. Then it seemed I heard a little noise — like a siren — then I noticed a red light on the hood, blinking! Yes, it was some kind of police. So I pulled over.

Three men jumped out! "What you been drinking?!" one shouted. I replied, "Nothing! I'm just a college student headed back to college! In fact I am a ministerial student, studying to be a preacher! Been home to see my father and mother!" While the first man seemed to be settling down, another had been searching the rear trunk, and came running around with his flashlight and exclaimed, loudly, "Preacher Boy, eh — what's this?!" he had found a whiskey bottle with my dad's homemade syrup in it!

I laughed loudly! The air was tense. I said, "Have a taste!" He did! He let out some words forbidden for a ministerial student to hear, "I'll be a @%#&#* — it is syrup!" We all laughed! Out on a lonely road, U.S. 41, in the dark of night! Tasting syrup out of a whiskey bottle! Is this funny nor not! What a relief. The officers became my instant friends and they led me back to a little motel where I spent three of my $104 for a room. I left early the next day.

## Diversion for an excursion

That is, to Grand Cayman Island, down below Cuba in the Caribbean. (Edna and I are on a Royal Caribbean cruise ship, "The Navigator of the Seas." I am writing this portion of the book while we are docked just outside the port. I'm sitting here in my shorts and T-shirt. I think I heard it announced that it is 81 degrees. Seven back in New York City, as the date is January 26. (Just thought you'd like to know — not that you'd want to be here!)

Deviation: I like to "deviate" when I am writing to give the reader an opportunity to travel with me. You see, this book is a journey and this little excursion is a "little journey" spinning off a journey! There is movement — lots of it — in my writings! Besides I think it is romantic — at least, it is to me. This was what I call "journal writing" as I mentioned in one of my previous books.

This cruise illustrates my theology — in the meeting of two beautiful persons, Daniela, from Italy, and Christopher, from Trinidad. Edna and I met Daniela at one of the dining rooms where she was a cute little waitress. I was sitting there with nothing to do except *be there* with my lapel badge which reads, "I Y Q". Daniela asked, "I Y Q?" I cut her off in the middle of her sentence and said, "Thank you, I Y Q, too!" Instant friends — communication deep into each other's spirit. Wow! Wonderful! I'd like to bring her home with us but Edna says we can't do that. We connected!

That's what's happening in the world today! People are being *drawn* together — in love throughout the world. It makes no difference what country, culture, language, race, religion — nor anything else! It's an *attraction* all over us, around us. Everywhere! What a privilege to be alive at such a time in history! Yes, life is a romance, a journey, a going somewhere! To where? To peace on earth, good will to men — a goal announced long ago by prophets, seers and angels!

Now, with the Internet, we can really get to know each other and truly enjoy our connection! Distance? What does that matter? We have instant communication via this spiritual gift of technology — from God who is bringing us together. He has other means just around the corner — awaiting discovery by creative minds! That's us!

At six a.m. today, Edna and I met Christopher, age 29, from Trinidad. Being early risers, we wandered down, looking for coffee. We found it — and Chris. For an hour we connected — the more we talked the more we discovered our *oneness*. He told me how the Muslim community in his native Trinidad "got along" with the Christian community! This struck a note with me, as it is my conviction that if we are to have peace in the world these two groups must find a way to co-exist, even become friends!

THERE'S ONLY ONE

## *AT-ONE-MENT!*

This is how I felt as I walked two miles on the ship's deck. As I gazed into the blue sky I thought, "I am a part of all this! I am at one with all this!" The wind blowing over me, those clouds floating above me, the azure blue out into infinity, the ocean, as far as you can see! Then these beautiful people I am meeting, and still meeting! Daniela has already led us to three or four others of her comrades aboard this ship! You might say, "There is something strange in the air!" Yes, there is! And it's beautiful. It's right here and now for each of us to experience and enjoy! Pam and Mike from Ohio overheard us *carrying on* with Daniela earlier this morning in the dining room, and I could tell they too are being drawn into whatever this is! They, like us, are *resonating* with the "sounds of the uni-verse!"

## *Let's back up — return 60 years*

To just north of where we were when I was stopped by the police! It's now the next day — the sun is up and I can see the road ahead! It's U.S. Hwy. 41 and I am atop Monteagle Mountain, about 50 miles north of Chattanooga. I'm in the clouds! Actually! Physically! The early morning fog is thick and I am covered — surrounded by it! I learned later that the only difference between fog and a cloud is fifty feet — if it starts fifty feet above the ground it is a cloud; if lower than fifty feet it is fog! So I am truly in the clouds! I don't know if I were on "cloud nine" as I did not count them! But one might say that, as I knew that Edna would be waiting for me just three hours away! I guess you might say I had a *vision* — of sugarplums dancing in my head!

## Back at Trevecca

It's still in my freshman year and I am assigned a new room and a new roommate — Carson Knowles. I think Carson was as poor as I! Each night we bought a loaf of bread, some mayonnaise and sardines! We mixed them together and imagined ourselves eating tuna fish! The room stank, and I think we did, too! We were playing a form of make believe.

## Breaking news from home!

The news came in the form of one of my sainted mother's weekly letters. To my astonishment, my father offered me a deal! If I would return home and work for him the three months of June, July and August, he would send me ten dollars per week for the remainder of the school year! This was good news from afar — seven hundred miles! I am thrilled! I can forget about having a job for the winter and spring quarters, focus on my schoolwork and have some quality time for this new girlfriend, fast becoming the love of my life!

Can the reader begin to see how a "Higher Power" than I is operative in my life and is actively bringing the dynamic forces of the universe together to create a beautiful romance — a real spiritual journey of this life you are reading about? I am hoping that the story of my life will give comfort and inspiration to others who face like circumstances.

Traveling note: Today we are docked in Ocho Rios (eight rivers), Jamaica. Beautiful small mountains surround the harbor and out the window is a Carnival cruise liner.

## *Back to Trevecca (Nashville, 1949)*

Summer arrives. Edna returns to her home in West Virginia. I took her to the Nashville airport where she boarded an old DC3. I'm off to Florida with two companions, who help pay for the gas.

The next day I pulled into the driveway of my dad's tourist camp. This time I was not concerned about being rejected as I was "under contract!" The seven-mile paper route was waiting for me and it was good to feel loose change in my pockets once again! Cash flow!

During July, Edna came down, flying on a DC3 again. I met her at the Daytona Beach airport and did we ever enjoy each other! One night we went to a drive-in movie where Edna enjoyed "The Wizard of Oz" and I enjoyed her! You know, sitting next to her in the front seat!

OSCAR POOLE

## *My sophomore year in college*

Summer has ended and my heart is pounding to see Edna! No trouble in leaving home this time — one year later! Edna awaits me in Charleston, West Virginia, where I am enrolled in Morris Harvey College, on the banks of the Kanawha River, directly across from the West Virginia Capitol building!

Edna's father, Harry Shock, agrees to pay me ten dollars per week to help him on his small farm. I picked up odd jobs, too, I guess because I was an "odd guy!" By now I was making all A's and B's and college work was getting easier.

I shall not forget in John Young's history class when an older student who was a member of the House of Delegates across the river at the capitol made a presentation of what he called, "The Seven Cycles of History" — that mankind was now in his seventh peak of civilization — his highest achievement on his upward progressive journey. The date was May 1950.

He pointed out that man (that's us) would either soar to unbelievable heights, or plunge to the deepest abyss of his existence, even lower than that of the cave man. All this he spoke 59 years ago!

Think of what has happened during this epoch of history: Television, tape recorders, traveling in space, cell phones, digital technology — I can call Moscow, Russia, from a small phone in my shirt pocket — and much, much more.

Yet, hate is strong and mocks the song of "peace on earth, goodwill to men!" I made good notes from this speech and preached it as a sermon, The Crisis of History! "Which way shall we go," I asked — the inspiration from the brilliant thesis spoken that day in a college sophomore class! As I enter my seventy-ninth year, the question still challenges me! I want to believe the way for mankind is *forever upward* — achieving greater miracles! I sit here aboard this cruise ship and ponder our journey! Sometimes I wonder, as I not only hear about "wars and rumors of wars", but find myself attending funerals of close, beloved friends who still die in battle! Who will ever forget 9/11 when a few pair of box-cutters brought America — the greatest power on earth — to our knees.

I am choosing the upward approach out beyond the imagination, even when my faith grows dim. Somehow we must find ways to solve our problems and bring about he desired ends of our spiritual leading gone before us — already stated in this book — of peace on earth, goodwill to men! Count me on the side of faith — this is the result of my Christian background and somehow hope continues to live inside me!

Want to know who the speaker was that day? Senator Robert C. Byrd, former Senate Majority Leader! Do you think I brushed against a little history that day? After all, it was a history class. Does this give some value to my college education? I think so! Sen. Byrd was a close friend of Edna's father and spoke at churches as a Gideon while Mr. Shock sang Christian solos. Mr. Byrd was also a friend of Glen and

Peggy Morton, Edna's niece, who prepared a meal and entertained a U.S. Senator, as well! I find these facts amazing as I live with this myself — Oscar Poole! I hope the reader can see a valid reason for the writing of this book — my experiences seem so real to me, interesting to say the least! My grandchildren might never know these things unless I write it!

## *Marriage to Edna — June 2, 1950*

Edna and I decided it was time to get married! After all, we had courted for almost two years. I am now a junior in college and Edna has completed high school. She is seventeen and I am the "not so ripe" old age of twenty. Edna's mother was not so happy about my becoming her son-in-law. In fact, she said we'd never make it! Well, we proved her wrong! Isn't it wonderful to prove mothers-in-law wrong?! It was for me! She finally gave in as she knew we'd run off anyway!

I'll never forget the night we were united in marriage! It was a Friday night – almost eight p.m. and here comes that song — "I Love You Truly", "Always", then "Because!" There we stood, up front! "Dum dum de dum — Here Comes The Bride" and there she was — coming down the aisle!

The song ended and Edna made that long journey. We faced the minister. He preached a little and asked a few questions, "Will thou (he spoke in Old English) have this woman to be thy lawful wedded wife?" I had no intention of violating any laws! I looked around to see which woman he was asking me to marry — there were so many beautiful women standing there — I wanted to get the right one!

I soon determined it was Edna he was talking about. She was beautiful! Radiant! We joined hands, said some words and headed down "life's highway!" This journey will soon make fifty-nine years!

## *Our honeymoon*

We left on our honeymoon — though, as I recall, there was no moon! It was cloudy. But Edna was my honey and she was sweet!

## *It's 1950*

We arrived in New Smyrna Beach where we spent the next two years on my dad's tourist camp! Now a married man! Little money, but lots of love!

The paper route resumed at fifty dollars per week. Up seven days at 4 a.m., then other odd jobs, e.g., two weeks at a gas station, church, work, work, work!

All summer we were planning to return to Trevecca Nazarene College. There was an old school bus someone lived in on the tourist camp. We considered buying it and taking it to Nashville so we could live in it and pursue my college career. That was not to be, as my father was feeling more secure about having his son back home! He talked me into inquiring about transferring my two years' college credits to Stetson University, in DeLand, a distance of 25 miles. I could commute, enjoy free rent, and keep my job!

# *John B. Stetson University*

You guessed it, I am now enrolled as a Junior at Stetson, a fully accredited university. I pursued two majors: one in religion and the other in English, plus a minor in history. All three would serve me well in years to come.

Our first home was a two-room cabin, Number 24. After a year we bought our first home-on-wheels, an 18-foot trailer. No bath, no refrigerator, only an icebox. A hand-pumped white gas stove to cook on. Not much of anything! But it was ours, and it was paid for! No mortgage payments. We paid cash for it. Notice that we are living out my conservative background! We had to walk fifty yards to a public bathroom. Of course, there was a nearby large bush!

Two persons, in love, working, attending university and having a good time doing it! It was romantic! What a learning experience — precious memories! Now, over half a century later, pausing aboard this ship, somewhere near Cuba —
 (I was just interrupted by Andressa, a crewmember from Rio de Janeiro, Brazil. We spoke briefly, as I shared with her I had visited her country diez (ten) times, playing the piano in most of the major cities!)

Let's get my college career over! June 1952 arrives and I received my first college degree — my Bachelor of Arts (BA). I am now twenty-two years of age, a married man with a college degree! Who would ever believe it?! Wow!

Oscar & Edna's First Home 1952

# Chapter VII
# Graduate School

Always, more! I am thirsting for knowledge. It is the fall of 1952, and Edna and I head for Kentucky — to Daniel Boone country. The place is Wilmore, just south of Lexington. I am continuing my studies in Greek, Philosophy and other fine arts. We had saved enough money for the first year's tuition, nearly that is! My father began to loan us enough to keep going for the two-year period of study. Oh, I forgot to tell you, it's Asbury Theological Seminary. At the time it was the haven for graduate study in the American frontier Holiness movement. Entire sanctification, the eradication of the old Adamic sin principle — but I never met anyone who had achieved it! At least I was exposed to this part of American culture. I enjoyed the studies and sat under some brilliant professors.

By now I was a good student, all A's and B's. This, too, was preparing me for further gradate study, years later. In fact, I enrolled at Pittsburgh University for a Ph.D. program, but during the summer of 1954 I decided I'd had enough, especially for now. I needed a rest from academic labors.

I received the Masters of Religious Education degree (M.R.E.) in May, 1954. I am now Oscar Poole, B.A., M.R.E. — my self-image is improving!

## *My first church, First Church of the Nazarene, Clarkson, Kentucky*

During August 1954, my friend D.D. Lewis, for whom our son, Darvin, is named, had the little Nazarene church "call" me as their pastor. I'll never forget the day we arrived to a brick church with stained glass windows, a parsonage next door, and forty dollars per week. Don't forget, I made fifty dollars a week back in high school with my paper route! Besides being conservative, we were frugal.

## *High School Glee Club*

Orin P. Lawlor, the county school superintendent, dropped by our house one day. He asked if I would consider directing the glee club, the high school chorus, for the school year 1954-55. What? Who? Me?! "I'm not qualified to be a high school vocal teacher," I said. But he thought otherwise! Word had gotten around that I played the piano and directed what little church choir we could muster. "I'll get you qualified," Mr. Lawlor replied. So we drove to Frankfort, Kentucky, the state's capital, and I got qualified with a one-year certificate. (For more details on this musical experience, please refer to my book, "I Hear Music!")

It's two weeks before school opens. I've got to perform! I'm not ready! In fact, fear came near me! What am I going to do? I selected a two-line hymn, "When I Survey," and approached Edna for advice. She had a couple of years background in a high school chorus. I said to Edna, "I know what this top note is — it's soprano, and this bottom note is bass, but what are these notes in between?" She replied, "Alto and tenor!" (I assume the reader knows there is a tremendous difference between piano music and vocal music.) I put together some "directives" that I thought might be a good direction to begin. It was — it worked! I placed the thirty-eight members into four section groups. I acted AS IF I knew what I was doing! I knew how to direct with my right arm. 2/4, 6/8, 3/4, 4/4 — I improvised the rest! I had learned directing in a two-hour semester course at Morris Harvey College.

In two weeks we went to the county fair and won first prize! The judges were from the prestigious Louisville Courier Journal. My principal, H.P. Lindsey, overheard one of them say, "That man knows what he is doing!"

The "glory" of this achievement was short-lived. The next day was Sunday. It is 10 a.m. and time for Sunday school to begin. I'm seated on the front row, when all *hell broke loose!* The leader spoke, "Our young people are going to Hell!" One member banged on a wooden pew and yelled, "No harm in going to a fair, I don't reckon!" I was shocked, stunned! I thought, *"What in the hell is going on?"* The song we had sung at the fair was "America." They sang beautifully, we were good! But, what is good?

## *Head-on confrontation with raw fundamentalism*

With an emerging liberal ... me! I was twenty-four years of age and barely out of graduate school. I did not know what to make of this.

I was caught in the middle. On the outside of the church I was a young, talented, successful high school teacher, but on the inside of my little church I was seen as "leading our youth to destruction." For the next two years, I had to cope with this! Constant tension and conflict permeated most conversations. I thought they should have been proud of me, but instead, there developed a religious hatred toward me. What was I to do? What could I do? I did what I advise others to do in such situation. I made the best of it! During the day I was a hero, on weekends, some sort of villain.

## *Edna, her clothes, her hair, her rings*

Once I stopped by Mrs. Badman's little gift shop in front of the post office to pick up some money for a paint brush, as I was painting both the church and parsonage — for free of course! I walked into her little back room, where she said, "Sit down, Brother Poole, I want to talk to you." So, Mr. Naïve sat down. I actually thought she was going to brag on me! Instead, she poured out her *pent up religious venom* on me. "Look at you," she exclaimed in a judging, condescending voice, "your sleeves are past your elbow! Your arm is practically naked, revealing your flesh!" I did not know that my flesh was sin! No one ever told me! But here I sat, for what seemed like an eternity.

After roasting me over the coals, she had some rather kind words to say about Edna, the young pastor's wife. "And there's Edna, your wife. We've never had a pastor's wife like her. She wears 'form-fitting' clothes," — I think she was referring to her wearing a bra! — "She cuts her hair! She wears a wedding ring!" Her raving finally came to an end and I went directly back to the house, where I shared with Edna what I just told you. Edna was devastated! I never saw her cry like that. The ensuing moments were worse than the confrontation at the little gift shop! By the way, Edna did take off her wedding ring, even though I never asked her to. Can you imagine the hurt Edna, the first lady of the church, experienced? Seeing her go through the treatment she received was truly difficult for me. I wondered if there was some way out of this mess.

One day, in 95-degree heat, Keith, our toddler of two years, was walking around the yard with no shirt on. Mrs. Badman's husband (the name was the opposite) stopped by to bring us some fresh vegetables from his garden. He ridiculed both the little boy, and of course, Edna and me, for allowing Keith's skin to show. I was beginning to wonder if I was the chaplain of an insane asylum!

One day the Sunday school superintendent who spoke the day following the county fair experience appeared in front of our little parsonage on an early Saturday morning as we were eating breakfast. I kept wondering why he sat in his green Chevrolet so long. So, I walked out to the car and inquired. He asked me to have a seat inside the automobile. He got right to the point. "God told me to come here and tell you that sin lieth at your door!" How do you deal with this? It's time for me to speak! "What sin?" I asked. "Did he tell you what sin it was?" It seemed to me that if God was speaking to him, that God would have been a little specific! Well, the specificity never came and he finally left. Now, it's early Saturday and time to prepare for a very spiritual weekend! Looking back, I often wonder what kind of sermon the people heard the next day!

Time is moving on. The bulk of two years is passing. My endurance level is wearing thin. What kept me sane during this time? I am sure it was the involvement in the school and community. It's as if I lived two lives! In 1955 it was my privilege to lead the countywide March of Dimes drive that broke all records — $5,800! This caught the attention of the state leaders in Louisville. A poor farming community, outdoing all the other surrounding areas.

## *Always look for the positive!*

Here are at least two positives — the Glee Club experience, and the March of Dimes. Well, let's not overlook the two years of coping with what I perceived as a bunch of lunatics!

Early 1956 arrives. I am asked by the Nazarene church officials to move to Lexington and start a new church with zero members! My heart was torn to even think of leaving my outside-the-church support system just mentioned. But the challenge excited me and off we went.

We rented the old Centenary Methodist church building on North Broadway. The building still stands. I saw it one month ago — it's just down the street from Rupp Stadium, where we attended a UK basketball game.

We spent the next six months as pastor of the Immanuel Church of the Nazarene right in the middle of downtown Lexington, Kentucky! Beautiful old church building with a great organ! I played it often.

Did you ever hear about "getting out of the pot and into the fire?" That is about what happened in this venture. We did attract about 40 dissidents from other Nazarene churches in the city — the pastors thanked me for getting them off their hands! Do you get the picture? A positive seeking young man thrown into the midst of another "den of lions!"

I'll make the report of this six-months brief — as we must get on with my life! The straw that broke the camel's back was when it was discovered that we took a Sunday paper. That was deemed "worldly" and it was taboo to have anything to do with reading a Sunday paper! I wish someone had told me that when I delivered 500 of them years earlier.

I need to mention that I taught one year of school at Bryan Station Junior High School during 1956-57. This was a totally positive experience!

The above-mentioned straw broke my back with the Nazarenes. So, we joined the Baptists!

Oscar is a favorite guest on many shows

# Chapter VIII
# Age 27 — The Baptists!

Leaving the people that I loved was not an easy experience. In fact, it was traumatic! I saw that I could not cope with such a strict legalism. I examined the "holiness" doctrine and since I could not find any "sanctified wholly" people, especially in church leadership, I looked toward the Baptists. I responded, "If Billy Graham can be a Baptist, I can, too!"

I made contacts. I sought counsel with my former professors at Stetson University, which was a Southern Baptist University. The main doctrines looked "historically correct" in terms of orthodox Christianity — salvation by faith — and others, so I took the plunge. Edna was with me and we were both baptized (again), by immersion of course. It all happened in Lexington, Kentucky. Soon I was ordained (again) and was "called" to be the pastor of the Southside Baptist Church in Richmond, Indiana — a "storefront" congregation. I got a job teaching school at nearby Abingdon. For a while, things settled down. We were successful! We improvised! We met at the church building and then drove cars loaded with youth to four homes, where we had classes. It worked! We grew! Denominational leaders began to take notice of us, and soon I was asked to serve on state committees for the purpose of forming a State Convention of Southern Baptists. We did! I personally wrote the motion that led to the official organization of Southern Baptists in Indiana. My friend, W.W. Rhody, now deceased, made the motion, I seconded it. It was adopted and I helped make history for Southern Baptists in Indiana.

## *A new church building*

During my two years stay with this new church we managed to build a new building — our own church home! I served as the general contractor, as I had some building experience. One day we had a large tub filled with water and there was a little hole at the top that was squirting out a steady stream of water. Darvin, our second son, who was born back at Clarkson, exclaimed to his mother, "Look, Mom! That tub is peeing!"

An insurance company took note of our achievement (national headquarters there in Richmond) and saw an opportunity to *cash in* on an insurance plan, which they called, "The Fellowship of Baptist Laymen." Each time a member passed away, every member would make a contribution to a fund that would help other new congregations building new churches. The Southern Baptist Convention, the national body, was promoting the building of 30,000 new churches throughout the country. The insurance company published a professional pamphlet, "We Built One of the 30,000!" This looked good on paper, and that's about as far as it got. But isn't it strange the variety of experiences coming Oscar's way?

The very day we entered our new building, I knew my work at Southside Church was over. I cannot explain how that very evening the vision and burden for that epoch in my life was ended. Even though we were apparently having a successful experience, being recognized by state and denominational leaders, it was over! A restlessness developed within me and remained with me for years to come.

## *The Oscar Poole Evangelistic Association*

We moved in November of 1958 into our new home in New Smyrna Beach. A home that my father paid $8,000 for and allowed us to make monthly payments — at no interest, I might add!

I organized the Oscar Poole Evangelistic Association and began traveling the country conducting revivals for Baptist churches. I was quite successful and enjoyed the hype that went into the events. And I was good at it! I thrilled at preaching to new crowds and being the guest evangelist! The only thing was that the evangelistic meetings were few and far between, and the family had to eat!

## *Back to Seminary*

I needed some additional education — especially at a Baptist seminary, if I am to really be successful at the evangelistic enterprise.

So after enrolling at the Southern Baptist Theological Seminary in Louisville, Kentucky, we packed up and Edna and I moved from our new home into an apartment at Seminary Village. Dewey Mann, the pastor of the First Baptist Church where I had "experienced God" at the age of three, paid the $150 for our moving fee aboard a ton and a half truck.

Off we go again! The day before we left I was able to sell a small business lot along U.S. Hwy. 1, just down the street from the place where I grew up, for $6,000! This paid off all debts owed to my father and there was $3,500 left to get us through one year of further graduate school.

The first semester my grades were three A's and one B. Now I had the attention of my professors and peers. The grading system was some kind of curve and after a couple of semesters several students were afraid to enroll in the same class with me! By now I am being looked at as an *intellectual!* Who me? This was both fun and exciting, besides, what it was doing to my self-image! It was like the A in Greek at Trevecca. Anyhow, it looked and felt good, so "things must be *right!*"

The Southern Seminary was viewed as the "Harvard" of Southern Baptists. They were the liberal version of Baptists. I was, in this regard, at the right place! What a great time I had for the next three years. I received a Bachelors degree in theology and a Masters degree in the same. I am now Oscar Poole, A.B., M.R.E., B.D. and M.Div. The degrees were bigger than my name — this looked good! Years later I returned for my doctorate.

## *The Elizabeth Baptist Church, 1960-61*

My senior year at Southern Seminary began in September. During the spring of 1960 a redheaded student asked if I'd "supply" at Elizabeth Baptist Church, a distance of 30 miles across the Ohio River. This I did. The people and I *took* to each other. They had me return the next Sunday and the congregation voted to extend me a call as pastor.

Within three months the church grew so rapidly the church board raised my salary to $100 per week! This included the rent on a fine farm home fit for a king!

My secret was knocking on doors! I visited everywhere. "Here comes that Baptist preacher!" The people liked it, a young pastor mixing and mingling with the people. My knuckles got sore, but I was learning the secret of my ministry — get out there and meet the people! I'd make fifteen to twenty pastoral calls per day and people would show up on Sunday!

I organized a choir and taught them to sing in parts, "making melody to the Lord!" It sounded good! Remember the glee club back in Clarkson? It served me well at Elizabeth. Of course, I played the piano and this resonated with the congregation. We were good for each other.

During the year our fourth son, Michael, was born on February 20, 1961. The school year moved right along, I was asked to deliver the commencement address at the local high school. Did I ever "sound off"! You'd think I was talking to the United States Congress! I gave a very *relevant* message on the theme of how I perceived our country was headed: "The Crisis of History!" Much of the essence of the message came from Senator Robert Byrd's speech that day in the history class back in Morris Harvey College ten years earlier! You can begin to see some of the *connectedness* of my life as I am

# There's Only One

moving forward on my spirit journey! I have delivered this address many times since.

What a glorious year this was! The entire Elizabeth experience was a spiritual package I needed! The congregation doubled! I had the most flourishing student-pastorate in theology school, made excellent grades and was gaining a healthy self-image. I think this latter was the greatest benefit. The people loved us, and we, the whole family, loved them! The church belonged to the American Baptist Convention — a different denomination from the Southern Baptists, of which Southern Seminary was a part. I mentioned earlier that Southern was the "more liberal" of all the Southern Baptist seminaries. The Elizabeth Church did not care whether a Christian could fall from grace! They just loved one another! It certainly was a far cry from the Clarkson congregation!

But that "restless spirit" I spoke of earlier began stirring! Coupled with a phone call from a pastor-friend in Florida, it added to another major change in our (all six of us!) lives.

Oscar Poole laughing at himself

# Chapter IX
# Methodists Calling — Age 31

"Can't this guy settle down?" I hear someone asking. Well, I've asked it myself — many times. Like Abraham Lincoln's father, every time we settled down, we moved!

The pastor friend who made the initial call reminded me that "at heart you are really a Methodist! There is more opportunity here in your own backyard — Florida!" So, I investigated and he was right. Darvin, age 5, and I made the exploratory trip to Florida in my Volkswagen, met with a committee of the Florida Conference of the Methodist Church, was offered an opportunity to pastor a congregation, and I accepted!

## *The Casselberry Community Methodist Church*

This was my next congregation. The year is 1961 and I am 31 years of age. I hit the road running. Knocking on doors. During the first year I made 1,800 pastoral visits. The O.M. Poole work ethic is appearing. There's that work-work-work thing again!

Did the people ever come! To church on Sunday, that is! Three to four hundred every Sunday — wow! The congregation was cosmopolitan — my kind! Don't forget I was raised in a cosmopolitan tourist environment just forty miles away at New Smyrna Beach! It was a *natural*. I spoke their language, and they mine. Amazing! I have found my *niche*. Everything works. We are leaders one again, out-doing everyone. At the end of the conference year, in June 1962, I walked down the aisle at Lakeland to receive my "Minister of the Year" award, and the church right behind me, received "Church of the Year" award.

Now what? Extreme popularity! Had the world by the tail on the downhill pull!

## *Something's not right*

In the midst of all this, something is not right! What is it? Almost everyone is bragging and affirming me and I am not satisfied. A deep, profound restlessness stirs inside! Is something wrong with me? Can't I stand success? Do I need conflict and tension to be a part of me? These were troubling questions. "You'll be pastor of First Church Tallahassee!" Words like that were spoken often to me. Who wanted that? Not I!

Parts of the Cassellberry experience were sheer delight! I loved the accolades, preaching to a packed house, the visiting in homes, but I saw *through* the establishment. I did not like what I saw — hypocrisy, politics, and much more. I guess I would be a good case for a psychiatrist. Or, could it be that some divine thread is leading me? This I have come to accept as subsequent years have unfolded. I resigned as pastor of the

Cassellberry congregation to return to Indiana to form a new church.

## *The Laconia Church*

A young, inexperienced pastor had followed me at the Elizabeth Church and a core group wanted to start a new church, with me as their pastor.

Here we go again!

About forty of us, all from the Elizabeth congregation, secured an old Presbyterian church building for $5 per week and began conducting services. The church was very stately, an old-fashioned wooden building out in the country. I mean *way out!* Every Sunday morning at 5 a.m., Keith, Darvin and I drove the two miles to build fires in the wood stoves. This is Indiana and does it get cold there! In fact, the coldest day I ever saw occurred there — thirty degrees below zero! And the next day it was twenty-five below. The high was zero! That happened during the week, so we did not have to close services the following Sunday.

It was like old times! That is, for a while. Within three months there were over one hundred in attendance. I did not mention that the Laconia church was fifteen miles south of the Elizabeth Church. Someone gave us an old school bus for a nursery. Improvising! Creative! Challenging! Inspiring!

But it was *too good* to last. After all these were Baptists, and that's what Baptists are good (or bad) for! Two ladies in the congregation started fussing over some trivial issue. Trivia attracts trivia — so it wasn't long until there was "lots of trivia" — an uproar! To make a long story shorter, we organized into a church, and turned it over to the Southern Baptist convention of Indiana that I helped organize a few years earlier. Let them have it — and they were glad to receive it!

## The Larchmont Church of God, 1963

Over in Louisville, 30 miles away, the internationally known minister, Ross Minkler, invited me to become his associate minister of youth and music. I accepted. These were the sophisticated "Church of God" people — the ones from Anderson, Indiana, who did not speak in tongues! This venture lasted for six months. The opportunity for advancement within their movement was open to me. In fact I was considered for their largest church in a metropolitan area of the state. But they "fussed," too. Crooked politics at the top — I was too intrinsically honest to give myself to that.

## The President Harry S. Truman story

I had a 15-minute private audience with Mr. President in his private office in Independence, Missouri. This took place sometime during 1962 when I was attending a preacher's convention in Kansas City.

## OSCAR POOLE

Here is how it happened! I was riding in the back seat with a group of ministers en route to Kansas City from Louisville, Kentucky, where I was an associate pastor to the quite well known Ross Minkler. We were assigned to staying in the homes of church members living in the area. I was assigned to a family in Independence. I casually asked, "Do you suppose while we are there that it would be possible for me to meet Harry Truman?" The unanimous response from the others present in the car was LOUD LAUGHTER! I can hear them now! WHA! WHA! "He would not have time to see you!" they said. (They sort of intimidated me into a "time of quietness!") I was somewhat embarrassed and kept my mouth shut! (Keep in mind that I am 32 years old at this time!) Why I ever raised the issue I do not remember.

We arrived at the convention center in downtown Kansas City. During the middle of one of the long, drawn-out boring sermons, I sneaked out to a pay phone. I called the Harry Truman Museum in Independence. I said to someone, "I'm an admirer of Mr. Truman, am visiting here from Kentucky, and wondering if I might meet the President." She replied, "Sometimes he meets visitors and if you'd come out here early in the morning, he might just see you!"

I had my answer: I CAN SEE THE PRESIDENT! I told no one. When early the next morning came, I was there! I met the security guard, making sure I made friends with him. The security guard said, "If you come over here to the side door about 7:45 — when he enters you can speak to him briefly — and maybe he will invite you into his office when he gets settled!"

Fifteen minutes later his personal secretary came out and said, "Mr. President will see you now!"

WOW! The next fifteen minutes I brushed history! I asked him questions about Josef Stalin, the atomic bomb decision in 1945 and other matters. What a thrill! I regret I did not have a camera with me! This became one of the highlights of my life and to this day I cherish the moments I spent privately with President Harry S. Truman!

I thought the reader might find this little anecdote interesting.

Oh, by the way, would you like to know what I said to my colleagues in the car as we left on our return trip to Louisville? I cleared my throat to get their attention — "Guess who I spent 15 minutes with the other day?! The man you said I couldn't see — Harry S. Truman!" Proving those guys wrong was as thrilling as meeting the President!

Personally, I think this experience may have influenced me in meeting so many famous people later. You might say, in this case, I STARTED AT THE TOP FIRST!

This is why I live in a "WHAT'S NEXT?" attitude! This is why I maintain that life, for me, is an ADVENTURE!

What does meeting President Truman have to do with being a pastor at Larchmont? Nothing! I just want you to know about one of my claims to fame!

OSCAR POOLE

## *First Methodist Church, Oakfield, New York, 1964–1967*

Anyone "give out" yet? It's time to move again! John Beeson, a friend since seminary days at Asbury, who had risen to the top amongst the Methodists in Western New York, convinced me that the grass was *greener* in those northern parts! Let's not forget the primary early influence in my life was those "Yankees" who lived on my Dad's tourist camp! It fared me well once again!

Prospects did look challenging and surely I can find myself with these people.

We loaded up, placed the doghouse atop our Cadillac and headed north — up through Pittsburgh, and northeastern Ohio, where they are famous for grapes and goat-milk fudge — on through Buffalo to Oakfield, four miles north of Batavia.

Can you imagine the scene when we drove up? Here is the new pastor, his wife and boys with a boxer dog on top of the car. It's the Beverly Hillbillies — no, it's the Rev. Oscar Poole Family! The entire congregation was out in the front yard enjoying their annual strawberry festival. It was Saturday and by church time the next day I managed to make about fifteen pastoral calls. I wanted to make a surprise entry by being in as many homes as possible, as soon as possible.

It worked! The people were impressed. That's because we were impressive! I'm not sure in what way.

Again, I *hit the road running*. The first full week I visited in fifty homes. No one had ever heard of this! It wasn't long until I had been in every home. Here's some more of that hard work ethic my father had given me, besides an obvious commitment. Within three months the church doubled in attendance. It was fun looking out the window of the parsonage next door each Sunday morning and watching the streets fill up with cars! I watched the church grow by counting the cars!

Word spread! And I just kept on working. I think I demonstrated that success is *within* the individual. Much of what was happening was almost oblivious to me and I had to stop and look at it to see the phenomenal success occurring. It came naturally. That's about the best way I can describe it. I was learning lessons in leadership — the best kind — where the shoe hits the road. Gaining insights, concluding principles of leadership and first hand experience. Difficult? Not really. Fun? Absolutely! I am here to tell you that being an "avant garde" person is truly exciting. Blazing new trails, entering where the brave dare not go! Discovering things that books are made of — later! (It's amazing how I see my life emerging as I am seated here at my Florida home writing about it!)

My tenure at Oakfield lasted three years, from 1964 to 1967. While there I became chairman of the Genesee County Ministerial Association and through it gained area acceptance beyond the denomination.

OSCAR POOLE

# A special service forever to be remembered!

This is quite a story — one I cannot, nor do I ever want to, forget. It happened at a summer youth camp at Silver Lake, just south of Buffalo. I witnessed the Spirit take control! It was out of my hands — even though I was the person in charge of an evening Vesper service. It was glorious! A "once in a lifetime" experience: to see fifty lives dramatically changed in a massive encounter with God! Beyond explanation, but I'll try to describe it.

The week leading up to the Thursday night experience was *dramatic* in itself. There were seven of us who served as the faculty to lead the camp. I was chosen to be music director, form a choir and be the evening speaker. There was tension among the faculty throughout the week. In one faculty meeting I raised the question, "Don't you think there ought to be an opportunity for commitment? Like coming to the altar and kneeling?" Paranoia set in amongst a few. They knew I was from the south and concluded that I was some kind of *fundamentalist* and that I had something up my sleeve — that I might pull off some kind of tear-jerking fiasco. "I don't want to have anything to do with any kind of emotional experience," one exclaimed. On one occasion I noticed a couple off to one side and knew they were discussing the matter I had barely suggested. Their fears were unfounded, as I had nothing like that in mind! In my opinion they were *northern elitists* who judged that if one was from the south, he had to be some kind of raving fundamentalist!

## There's Only One

At the last moment, on Thursday afternoon, I said to a team-member who was very much in support of what he thought I wanted to do, "I think I'll drop the whole idea!" He said to me, "Oscar, if you do, I'll punch you right in the face!" A little exaggeration! Don had been discussing the matter with two others and was trying to explain to them what I had proposed to do might be a good thing. I did not know this — that there was a positive emerging drama going on and I was in the middle of it. During the last faculty meeting one member said, "We've asked Oscar to do a job. We're telling him what to do!" This seemed to make some sense and that's the way it was left. Little did they know that I was trying to back out!

Thursday evening came. It was time for Vespers. There seemed to be an aura, a presence surrounding us. I had been speaking love and affirmation to these kids all week and they were resonating! I had said nothing of the traditional terms of "getting saved" or of "hell" — I simply spoke loving affirmation. Simple, soft-spoken words. My colleagues had built up an idea that simply did not exist. But we've all done that.

It's time for my little eulogy! I spoke for twenty minutes about how much they meant to their parents, their family and to their friends, and to God! They listened! You could hear a pin drop.

About two-thirds through my brief message, I heard a teenage girl to my left begin a small sniffle of a cry. I said to myself — or to God inside me — "Oh no! Don't let this happen! I don't want there to be anything emotional!"

## Oscar Poole

Another over to my right started a little cry! I'm trapped! I hurried up and brought my remarks to a conclusion. Then I gave what I felt was a very broad invitation. I had the lights turned low with candles lighted and had the organist play softly. I invited all who were there to come to the altar and simply meditate. "Maybe you want to talk to God in a conversational way. Or you just want to think!"

I led the way by kneeling myself, only for two or three minutes. When I got up I saw that the entire audience of about fifty youth had followed me! I went to my room and turned them over to the six other counselors, who had their hands full — of one of the greatest situations a group of spiritual advisors could ever have. All positive! Open! Free! The kids asked questions about life and God that only kids can ask! Openness and loving honesty prevailed. The counselors, all of them, loved it! One of those teenagers was Carol Anne Bo from Rochester. She later became a missionary to France and we are friends to this day, forty-three years later!

After a few minutes I left my room and came out into the yard where the service was still *spilling* over! There were expressions of joy and excitement — the likes of which I have never seen, even to this day. The greatest spiritual event of my life! I witnessed a body of youth, ages 13, 14, and 15, encounter God! I don't know how else to put it! While meandering out under the trees, one girl cried openly, almost embarrassingly! Dick Claussen tapped her on the shoulder and asked, "What's wrong?" She turned around and literally shouted in his face, "Nothing's wrong! For the first time in my life, everything's right!" One young man came up to me and said, "Mr. Poole, you make me want to be a Christian!"

The speech was joyous, electrifying! None of the old fundamentalist jargon the counselors had feared. Simple everyday expressions right out of their hearts!

Within a half hour or so the enthusiasm on the campus subsided and we all went to our rooms. The three other male counselors gathered round my bed and did we ever have a high time! One counselor put his hand out to me — I'll never forget, he had a big hand — "You're not a fundamentalist!" He said. The next morning it was time to return to our homes. Edna and I were having lunch. We had hardly finished when the phone rang. It was Bob Root, my district superintendent in nearby Batavia. "I want to come see you and talk to you about last night," he disclosed. My heart sank! I'm in for it now, I thought to myself.

Within thirty minutes Bob arrived. We sat at the kitchen table. He asked, "Where did you receive your sermon training?" I staggered out a few responses. I still didn't get the direction of where our discussion was heading.

Word had gotten out over the western New York conference about the great service we experienced the night before. All positive! For one thing, I earned my wings as some kind of great preacher in the western New York area! Who me? Well, it was not I, but the inner presence of the I Am God residing in me! I was more surprised than anyone else! While at the table, Bob poured out affirmations and accolades! Here I am seated in the kitchen of the parsonage listening to myself being praised for something I felt I wasn't even responsible for! I still, to this day, know it. But I am humbly thankful for having witnessed first hand a sovereign move of God, which I'll never forget!

## *The Cabin on Sodus Bay (The Piano Story)*

After we had been at Oakfield a year, there came an opportunity to bid on old houses on a large piece of property that the Federal Government was making into an Indian Reservation. Rumor was you could bid $25 and purchase most any of the houses. I found a cute bungalow and bid $36.01 for it — and won the bid!

Several church members joined in with me and we dismantled the little house and moved it to Sodus Bay, thirty miles east of Rochester, to a small lot on Eagle Island, which we had purchased. I built a homemade pontoon raft for hauling supplies across the half-mile bay, which separated the island from the mainland.

Someone gave me an old piano for the cottage. How do you get it across the water? That's simple! Just put it on top of the homemade rig and pull it across! Five men helped me load the piano onto the little barge. They got into two other boats with one of them attached to the raft. I sat behind the piano precariously. So, what does one do seated behind a piano? He *plays* it! You need music in the background when you do such a thing! By the way, the barge cost $1.25, the cost of wire used to connect the steel barrels to the frame — *conservative* values!

Six months later at a restaurant in Kodak Park, Greg and I sat eating at the small bar next to a man who exclaimed, "I fish down there at Sodus Bay. Let me tell you. The strangest thing happened there while I was fishing a while back. We were fishing out in the lake. We heard music! Here came a small barge and a man was playing the piano on it!" I said, "That was me!" I loved playing that piano to invited guests who came to see us.

## *The God-is-Dead Series*

During 1965 there was a "God Is Dead" propaganda going around the country. One of the five theologians promoting it was a seminary professor thirty-five miles away at the Colgate-Rochester Divinity School where many of the western New York Methodist ministers were trained. Another of the five was from the Chandler School of Theology of Emory University back home in Georgia. It looks like I am somehow going to serve as a link between the two! Can't believe this — I seem to walk into so many different *strange* situations. Now I know that I *attract* them! I did not know then of quantum physics or nano technology.

I got angry and decided to preach a series for five weeks on the subject. I did it to ridicule what we were hearing in the news. I ran articles in the Batavia newspaper: God-Is-Dead! One outstanding family came from Batavia to straighten me out — and joined the church! They became powerful spiritual leaders in the Oakfield church and some of my closest friends. I published my sermon notes in our church newsletter and discovered they were used for discussions in a class of theology at the seminary. How did I ever get into this?! While as a young inexperienced preacher I was intimidated then, I am proud of it now! This was one of the big surprises to come my way during the three years at Oakfield.

## *Other tidbits at Oakfield*

While we were there Edna joined a bowling team. One night per week she played on a team in Batavia.

I'm always playing tricks! One night around midnight Edna tip-toed into our upstairs bedroom, not to awaken anyone. As she pulled the string for the light to come on in the walk-in-closet, there I stood!

Another time Edna came in quietly I had placed the pillows to look as if I were in the bed, but I was under the bed! Just having fun! Playing tricks. Now that I am older I would not do the two things just listed — I have more sense! It's a wonder Edna did not kill me!

## *Michael and his chocolate milk*

One day our son, Michael, who was five years old at the time, was riding his tricycle next door at the Hensel's drive-in dairy. Harold drove in and out the driveway delivering milk. Of course, it was an area where little boys could ride their tricycles, especially little ones from next door! "I sure wish I had a bottle of chocolate milk," he said as he pedaled himself around. Michael never looked at Harold. You know what happened! Not only one bottle, but chocolate milk became readily available! Forty-five years later I wonder if Michael loves chocolate milk.

We bought new living room furniture and Edna told our four sons they must never sit on the couch in their play clothes. It was a Sunday morning. We were getting ready to go next door for church. There they sat, all four of them, dressed in their Sunday best.

We had a great three years at Oakfield from 1964 to 1967. The whole family was much involved and there are many more stories that could be told! Never a dull moment! Lots of adventure! It could easily compare with Andy Griffith's movie, "Angel in My Pocket."

What a time we had! As I look back, these were outstanding times. They were simple and innocent, fun loving, memories one can be proud of!

## "You can have anything you want!"

One day I was riding in the car with Bob Root, our district superintendent. Bob said to me, "Oscar, you can have anything you want in this conference!" (The Western New York Conference.) He was trying to settle me down into remaining with these New York folks. He meant that if I stayed with them I could have any church I wanted. How do you suppose such a statement made a 37-year-old young minister feel? Actually it had a humbling effect upon me. Often I have wished I had stayed with these people and found out what Bob was talking about. Bob had picked up on a rumor that there was a small group in Texas that had been making overtures for me to organize a community church in Fort Worth.

Two months before moving to Texas, our church hosted the first Lay Witness Mission in the whole state of New York. Who should lead this newest venture in church evangelism but Ben Johnson himself — the founder of what many were calling an *avant garde* approach for a local church reaching out into its community. I had known Ben Johnson from earlier days back at Louisville and Elizabeth.

The three-day weekend consisted of laymen coming in from neighboring churches — some near and some not so near. A few came from New York City, from Vincent Peale's Marble Collegiate Church who was still alive and active during this time. All of the material I am presently sharing with you seems like a fairy tale now that I look back at it!

## *The E. Stanley Jones experience*

One more episode before we leave for Texas! The entire Western New York Conference hosted a youth rally and called in an 84-year-old to be the keynote speaker, but it was not just any 84-year-old. It was the famed E. Stanley Jones.

Who did they ask to lead the singing? You guessed it, me! I was the only one who knew the hymns with which E. Stanley was familiar — even though the hymns were included in their own Methodist hymnals! Anything to do with an intimate personal relationship with God had been ignored for a generation! I had to teach them their own hymns! I was surprised at this!

I spent one hour with Jones in the church parsonage preceding the evening service. It's one hour I'll never forget! An hour with the man who spent ten days with Mahatma Gandhi! Another wow! Jones had given his life as a missionary to the *intellectuals* of India! He and I resonated! We had much in common. He was very much at home with the theology for which I was searching. We *connected!*

What is the significance of all this? Not only was I brushing history in meeting Jones, there was a connectedness, a *divine synchronicity* at work. I see the principle of association — like attracts like! And I feel pretty good about it! Even now, some 43 years later, it strengthens my self-image. Occasionally I find myself needing to be reminded! I guess it has taken all these years for my theology (understanding of life and spiritual things) to develop. I call this *devolution* — to more fully grasp what really happened back then. I understand this to be *progressive revelation* — that God reveals himself in and through us progressively! I see this progressiveness at work within me continually! I believe this is what many psychologists mean when they say life is a continual learning experience. What we encounter throughout life often may not be fully understood until later. This, I am sure, is my rationale for change! Like moving water, when it becomes still or stagnant, stinks! It's the same with beliefs. Stagnant truth is just

## Oscar Poole

that. What is *fresh* in one generation becomes *stagnant* in another. Well, I see I've gone to preaching. The Jones affair was something else! It exceeds the meeting with President Harry Truman earlier!

Note: Exclamation Marks! As I read this material I see that I am using a lot of exclamation points. I am expressing myself in this way because that's how I've lived — excitedly! Also, the reader will note that on occasion I place the sequence of my life "on hold" and tell of an immediate experience while writing it. I try to keep it "related." At lease, I am *unique* — "there's only one Oscar Poole!"

The Famous Col. Poole's Georgia Bar-B-Q

There's Only One

Oscar Broadcasting Radio Shows

Newt Gingrich, Pete Castello

# Chapter X
# The Texas Excursion

## *An interlude of two years, 1967-69*

We're not through with the Methodists yet — but we need to leave Oakfield and travel to Texas for an interlude of two years while we build a community church congregation.

During our last couple of years at Oakfield, I met J. C. Sullivan, former gangster-turned-preacher, who was amenable to starting a new church in the Dallas/Ft. Worth metro area. Being the eclectic that I am, drawing truth from many sources, I had early in my formative years favored an interdenominational, or better, a non-denominational approach to *Christendom*. Why not take the best from each tradition, enjoying the contributions of all segments of Christianity into one body of believers. My idea was much like the federated church that E. Stanley Jones had proposed.

## *So, off we go!*

This time, Box, our "spiritual dog," did not ride atop the car! Instead, he rode up front with Oscar driving a U-Haul truck. Edna and our four sons spent six weeks at her home in Charleston, West Virginia, while Box and I prepared a place for the family to come later.

# There's Only One

It's hot — I mean, hot! But we made the trip successfully — Box, myself, and all of our earthly goods. We arrived at the home of J. C. Sullivan, a lovely estate at the city of Colleyville, about 10 miles northeast of Ft. Worth.

On the second day, after only one night's sleep, Nellie, J.C.'s wife, said to me, "Lin Wright lives over here *about a mile* and he said he would like to meet you!" I wasted no time in getting over there!

I arrived at Lin and Martha's house where we had an old fashioned Texas breakfast together! We visited for about two hours, eating and *having a good time* — what else? When Lin announced, "We're going to join your church, all four of us!" What? I haven't been here 24 hours, don't even have a church, and the first four members join! Surely, this is a *right* thing!

"Oh, by the way," Lin said, "We have this house with three bedrooms and two baths right over here beside the runway and you can move into it until you work out *permanent plans!* Wow again!

In a short time we had the truck unloaded and went to work painting the house throughout — the house we were to live in for the next full year while we arranged to have our own home built. I called Edna to tell her the news — less than 24 hours after Box and I had arrived, we have our home secured, for free, and four new members. And we haven't been here a full day!

## Oscar Poole

Oh, I forgot to tell you that three other families were moving from Oakfield with us to start this new church! The Ingrahams (Bob served as my associate), Alice and Dick Goode, and the Sanders — there were eight of them — so let's add them up! A total of twenty members! No church building! No church budget! No salary! Only a vision — now shared by twenty people!

During these six weeks we found a little place to meet, a small office at Blue Bonnet Hills, overlooking a cemetery where you could see both downtown Dallas and Ft. Worth.

Also, during these six weeks, I met the Grimsleys near Lake Charles, Louisiana, where I was serving as music director for an interdenominational *camp meeting*. I shared my vision for a community church, and they joined! Five hundred miles away though they lived just outside Colleyville! More *divine synchronicity?* I think so! Now we have 23 members! It seems we are falling over ourselves and coming up smelling nicely!

Within a few days two other families called from nearby Grapevine, Texas, and came over to see me. They had heard about our plans to start a new church. I explained to them our vision and they, too, decided to join! Now we had eight families coming together and we have not had our first service!

I went back to West Virginia to get the family. We traveled to Florida to visit a few days with my father and mother. Then on to Texas in our non-air conditioned car. The month was August. We traveled through 95 and 100 degree temperatures. It was so hot we planned all our stops at air-conditioned restaurants, mainly to cool off!

## *Our opening service*

The time came for our new church to begin. The day arrived. The three families from New York had moved down and purchased their homes.

We placed our piano in the little office, found some folding chairs and on the Saturday night before "set up" for our *inaugural* service! Forty persons gathered into that little place! Among them was a Mr. Wimpy, the PR man for the "richest man in the world" — the famed H.L. Hunt! I was impressed! First service! A connection with the richest man in the world! I must confess I saw dollar signs in my head! But that was as far as that source of money went. An association with the Hunt family did not develop and that was the end of that scenario. I found out later that while I was somewhat conservative, I was not "right-wing" enough! That connection could have led into dangerous waters I did not want to tread!

The congregation grew! Fifty. Sixty. Seventy! We had to have more room! The local elementary school was across the street and we managed to rent the cafeteria and use their restrooms. We began to fill up our new spacious meeting place and talk emerged of building our own church. We named our church "People's Church" — after Oswald Smith's famed church in Toronto, Canada. We began a radio program over KSKY in Dallas. Our theme song was the Mormon Tabernacle Choir's *Battle Hymn of the Republic!* We sounded good! Bob and I! A new church in the Dallas/Ft. Worth area with two young preachers from New York!

One day Polly Benson showed up! She, with the Lin Wrights, remain strong friends of ours until this day!

We started out with a BANG! We grew to nearly a hundred. But the "big bang" was not to last. A charismatic element came into our midst, and I was unprepared for the *theological and practical* skirmishes that began to ensue. You got it: church fusses emerged. Before long I began to be unsure of my being an *eclectic* and decided that life within organized religion wasn't so bad after all!

## *"When you create a new goal*

You set up the opportunity for tension and conflict!" So said Robert Schuller. But I had not heard him say this until years later. I did not know this, but at the time I did not realize that what we were experiencing was creative conflict! While I did not see People's Church through to its desired ends, I feel quite qualified — from my Texas experience — to share with the reader some of the *practical dynamics* of "Charismania" in this country, especially as it relates to *traditional* expressions.

During the second year of my "attempt at leading a divided congregation" I made contacts with my friends back in Georgia — you guessed it! They were Methodists!

## There's Only One

One day the bishop, John Owen Smith, called me. I'll never forget! It was a voice from heaven! That South Carolina drawl — "Oscar, you still want to come to Georgia?!" "I sure do, Bishop!" I handed the People's Church over to Bob, my associate, and began to make plans to move to Georgia — to the Promised Land! By now, age 39, I had learned how to be successful as a pastor of a congregation. The Methodists had heard about this "success image" and wanted me! Little did they know that inside I felt defeated.

Oscar's First Bar-B-Q

# Chapter XI
# Back To The Methodists

We "loaded up!" Edna's dad, Harry Shock, often said that when our chickens heard a truck coming, they "laid over for their legs to be tied!" Instead, we placed them in a cage on the back of a trailer that we pulled all the way to Hiram, Georgia, about 30 miles west of Atlanta, where we'd "camp out" for the next 12 months. I say *camp out* because we are not going to stay here, either!

## *A word about tension and conflict*

As I look back about the Texas experience I see it as sort of a sidetrack in my life's journey, although I think it was a necessary part. The word *fight* is really not in my vocabulary, as it is not a *part of my nature.* I have learned, as David Hawkins has pointed out, "Love is the *greatest* force in the world!" I have always seen *church-fighting* as in-fighting and I ask, "Why fight in the first place?!" Did not those folks, back when I was three to five, tell me that since God is love, that we should love one another? I see I have opened a can of worms that I really have *no interest* in!

But here we are! In Georgia — that "Promised Land!"

About those chickens on the rear of our entourage! They belonged to Keith, our eldest son. Can you believe what was about 400 feet from the country church we were moving into? Chicken houses full of chickens, about three or four thousand! So, our adding four or five more was not really significant, except that we built a little chicken pen too near the house we were to move into. It later caused a murmuring by a disgruntled church member. How dare our minister bring in four or five more chickens adding to the 3,000 or 4,000 we already have!

A few hours earlier, while passing through Birmingham, one of Keith's chickens laid an egg! Someone came up beside us at a traffic light and exclaimed, "Your chicken just laid an egg back there!" That's the first time anyone ever gathered eggs on the road in downtown Birmingham!

We have landed! A crowd of 15 to 20 are waiting for us. It's 11 p.m. at night! Can you imagine the sight? We are like Jacob's family arriving at Pharoah's house at Cairo, Egypt! I see nothing wrong with the *resemblance* — after all, we wanted to be *biblical!*

## *Pastoral visitation*

Began immediately! One day I was out visiting in the neighborhood. There I was, standing with a couple of ladies in their front yard. I felt something warm on my lower left leg. I looked around and there stood a large dog, enjoying relieving himself with his leg lifted up to mine! I do not remember *what* was said, nor *if* they saw what happened! I do remember that it became one of my *shortest* home visits ever! No, the dog did not come to church the next Sunday!

OSCAR POOLE

## *Operation Involvement*

During the year (1969-70) we put together a special weekend experience. In cooperation with the Institute of Church Renewal in Atlanta (Ben Johnson, President, the very same man who led our Lay Witness Weekend back in New York), we brought together several agencies from the community: the department of family and children services, the county court system, the sheriff's department, the school system and the juvenile court. We sat down in general meetings, smaller groups, and took field trips with the various agencies. Church members were hosted by community leaders. Some visited in needy homes, some rode with police in squad cars, some visited in jails and made friends with the inmates. The idea was to get the church *out of the church* and minister to a hurting world!

It worked! At the end of the weekend experience a final general meeting was conducted and plans made for practical ministries beyond. Every Monday afternoon schoolbusses brought students needing help with reading and their studies to the church building. The Bethel United Methodist Church, a country church! A *country church* doing city things! Leading the way! Blazing new trails!

The district superintendent had me write it up and it was placed in one of the United Methodist national publications, *Tydings*, 1971, as "one of the *most creative* and *innovative* ministries" within the United Methodist Church!

THERE'S ONLY ONE

## *Lordy, Lordy, Oscar turns 40!*

On April 29, 1970, during the one year we were at Hiram, we greeted my fortieth birthday! I'm finding myself, but not in the traditional terms of the "way we always did it!" Naturally, there was conflict arising in the congregation about "those dingy children *dirtying up* our beautiful church!"

I'd had enough of this "___" (you supply the word!) The idea of teaching in a college or university began to appeal to me, as I was *good* at teaching, and this would get me out of the fighting of local churches! The *inside* turmoil I experienced within the confines of organized religion appalled me! It *sickened* me! I simply could not *stand it!* It robbed me of all the joy that *came* my way — a phrase I have learned from *quantum physics* — in spite of the volumes of time spent attending to *trivial issues* and busy-body in-fighting!

Is there anything better than this? After nearly 20 years, I am looking for a way out! I left Hiram in June 1970, built two cabins overlooking Blue Ridge Lake near Blue Ridge, Georgia. Our two sons, Keith and Darvin, and their younger brothers, Greg and Michael, helped, too! We built these cabins to raise a little money to live on and to make our move to Lexington, Kentucky, in pursuit of a Ph.D. at the University of Kentucky! It was a *good* idea, but not the *right* one!

We stayed in Lexington less than one week — arriving on Saturday and by the next Wednesday we were loaded up, ready to return to Georgia! Oh, yes! The chickens were in their nesting place on the rear of the trailer. We parked out front of the church, the Smiley Memorial Community Church on Richmond Road. It was a Wednesday night service and I preached my "farewell sermon" before returning to Georgia! Tom May, my beloved pastor-friend, prayed a *closing prayer* and got to laughing as he was praying — aloud! "And don't let the wheel fall off the chariot as they journey back to Georgia!" Immediately after his prayer he said to me (privately), "Oscar, get out of here and don't you ever come back!"

## *A traumatic experience — Box died!*

While there in Lexington our family pet, Box, who rode atop the car to New York and in the truck to Texas, decided he had "had enough" and left us. Actually it was not quite like that! In an act of love, while straining himself under a chain fence, trying to reach us, Box ripped inside muscles, bleeding ensued, and we buried him out back at Tom's church! The whole family experienced some kind of catharsis as we received God's love through our loving family pet! I wrote this into a sermon I entitled, "Boxer Dog Theology" — came back to one of our cabins and preached it the very next week at the Blue Ridge United Methodist Church, where a lady had just lost her family pet that very week and was in the process of grieving! Some more of that *divine synchronicity* I spoke of earlier? I don't think so — I know so! Just a few weeks ago, Herb Outlaw's son, Mark, who serves as a pastor in the North Georgia Conference of the United Methodist Church, told me the "one thing I remember about you is that Boxer-dog sermon you preached! I've shared it many times!" This 39 years later! Lasting "precious memories"! My heart is *touched* again as I think of it now. I even "feel the pain!"

## *Back in Georgia, 1970*

We moved our belongings into one of the small cabins we had built that summer! It is late August. I am 40 and here we are! Right where we are supposed to be! We still are as our story proceeds!

I soon got a job teaching junior high school at Mineral Bluff, Georgia, just three miles from where La Vie now stands — twelve choice acres of mountain land *given* to us for a retreat center!

Our boys all enrolled in local schools. Keith graduated from Morganton High School as a co-valedictorian! His address was entitled, "Being Led By The Spirit." I wonder if he thought his father was any kind of a model?!

Keith excelled in his spiritual development that year. Renee Outlaw, the sweetest teenage girl I have ever known — next to Edna, of course — came into Keith's (and our) lives! She was a powerhouse! Dynamic! Spiritually beautiful! I wish she lived next door now!

OSCAR POOLE

## *Over half-way, 1970*

That is, from 1930 until now — 2009! In terms of years, that is! I am now 79 years of age and the book thus far has reported to 40! How many left? No one knows, but I have "put in" for 45 more, 'til age 124! I need that many years to accomplish the *goals* and *dreams* deeply embedded within me!

THERE'S ONLY ONE

Col. Poole's Georgia Bar-B-Q

- 134 -

OSCAR POOLE

# Chapter XII
# Gilmer County — 1971-75

We're not through wandering! Although we are about to sojourn four — I said four full years in one place — to Gilmer County, Georgia, 75 miles north of Atlanta, in the town of Ellijay. These are without a doubt, our best four years of real ministry!

It is June 1971. Annual Conference is approaching and time to make appointments in the United Methodist Church! I went to see Charles Middlebrooks, superintendent of the Dalton District. It was a Sunday noon and he told me about a "circuit" of four little churches over in the next county, Gilmer. "Drive over and take a look and see what you think! In the meantime I might find something else a little closer to Atlanta!"

My heart sank! Here I am, 40 and I'm having to start all over! The salary was that of a college student. I have a family and the salary was $4,000, combined from all four churches! I found out later that no one wanted to be pastor. It was way off in the corner of the world. The only plumbing was outhouses!

But within minutes, my heart rose — I was normal again and an *inner voice* began to speak! "Man's worst could be God's best!" I actually heard that — deep inside me! I kept hearing it as Edna and I drove to Ellijay that evening and visited the four churches — Cartecay, that had been used as a hospital in the Civil War, some eight miles east of the little mountain town of

Ellijay; Cochran, at the top of Corbin Hill within the city limits of Ellijay (attendance was 10 to 15); and two other churches west of Ellijay, Nine Mile Church, that sat "on a hill far away," and Gates Chapel. They were all nestled in some of the most beautiful mountain country of North Georgia! Quaint! Simple! Just waiting for someone to come along and love on them! That I could do — and did for the next four years!

Here our family blended in with their peers. Keith enrolled at nearby Young Harris College, and Darvin graduated from Gilmer High School where he stood out in football and in the school glee club — following in his dad's footsteps!

Within one month I had visited in all of the homes of the members! I found them right where they were — milking cows, plowing their fields, and eating those North Georgia biscuits and sorghum!

Once we had a combined prayer breakfast with 75 in attendance at the prestigious Top O' Ellijay Restaurant, overlooking the scenic town of Ellijay. A camaraderie began to emerge. "We are somebody! We can do what others do!" It was a beautiful spirit. Love flowed! Attendance grew! This had never happened in the people's memory! But it was true. Full houses of worship! Excitement amongst the people!

We began to do as many things together as possible.

We conducted a "tents" revival meeting in the center of Ellijay. We placed four funeral tents side by side with a boy scout tent for a volunteer choir of about twenty persons (guess who the director was?!). Tom May from Kentucky was our guest preacher. The attendance averaged 150 per night. The new district superintendent, Dr. H. Dan Rice, dropped by for an evening service and couldn't believe what he saw! I think this first impression set the tone for the ensuing four years. Once Dan said to me, "Oscar, you are Mr. Methodist in this county and whatever you say goes!" How is that for building self confidence in this emerging spiritual leader?

We quit having frivolous board (bored) meetings! We went 13 months without having a single one! We conducted church business on the run! And run we did! In four years we led the Dalton District with 100 new members! We raised, for all purposes, over $350,000, built one new church building, organized the Gilmer Parish — a new concept in small churches working together. I was able to convince the leaders that we were not four separate churches — but one church meeting in four places! Word began to spread throughout the state conference about what was happening "up in Gilmer County!" In fact, twenty-five of the parish members traveled down to the annual conference where they were asked to come down front and receive their accolades as the "Church with Merit" for 1974-75! Can you image how these folks felt as they sat there on the campus of Emory University awaiting their commendation from the bishop! It thrills me to relive the event as I write about it!

## *Doing ... then writing*

I think this is one of the most *significant* concept/dynamics discovered throughout the Gilmer experience. Most people are looking for what they are "about to do" in the wrong places ... books, or studies, when they should be looking *within* themselves, coupled with the need they are facing. In fact, this is how the Bible was written! They did it first — then wrote about what they did! In other words, history came before theology! This seems *so obvious* to me!

In the Gilmer project we developed sort of a DAPDAE scenario —
  **Data**: Get all the facts
  **Analyze the data**: What do these facts mean?
  **Plan**: Develop a plan of action
  **Delegate**: Assign others to help you with specific tasks
  **Action**: Just do it!
  **Evaluate**: Summarize, draw conclusions

This *sophisticated* approach developed as we went along! I think this philosophy has something to offer others who are facing obstacles or needing to get things done! You lead by precept and example! You could call it *modeling*. You *show* people the way — don't tell them! Who knows, they might have a better way than the way you did it! Wouldn't that be frightening? I think it would be a compliment!

## OSCAR POOLE

This raises some serious questions about the writing of the Bible. Do you think there might — just might — be a better way of approaching some the problems the Apostle Paul faced in some of his troubled churches, e.g., the Corinthians and women speaking in public meetings. Just asking! I really never thought of it this way until this moment! Another new way of looking at things — even the Bible — in this new age. After all, it has been a full age of over 2,000 years since the New Testament was inspired! Now that I have written this statement, is it scripture (escribir — to write)? It is written at 5 a.m. and I do feel a sense of inspiration! I wonder what comments this declarative sentence will bring forth. I see "I've gone to thinking" out loud!

It came time for Darvin to graduate from high school. It was 1973 and we had been in Gilmer County two full years! An accomplishment in itself! I remember well the night of Darvin's graduation as he received the "I Dare You Award!" The principal spoke to me a few moments after the commencement service at the Gilmer High football field, "Mr. Poole, I have a son and when he grows up I want him to be just like your son, Darvin!" Of course, tears came into my eyes! What an accolade! How would you feel? Proud, just like his mother, Edna and me! These are moments too precious to forget! By the way, Darvin is now retired as a successful high school math teacher and coach. He and Greg are managers of Col. Poole's Georgia BAR-B-Q, Inc., carrying on a family legend in the very county where they grew up!

Another "by they way!" We were having a little trouble with Greg, our number three son, getting serious about his school work. So one day I spoke with Greg, "That's alright, you don't have to go to college like Keith and Darvin — all work is honorable and you could get a job at a gas station, work hard, save your money, and be successful!" Greg took this discussion seriously! He got somewhat angry and said to himself, "I'll show him!" He began making all A's and B's and later earned both his Bachelor of Science degree and a very prestigious M.B.A. — the Master of Business Administration degree. He has for years been a highly successful employee of a major trucking firm. Greg says I was "pulling some reverse psychology" on him and now I can tell that he was right — even though I did not realize it!

Where's Michael, son number four in all this? We'll save him until Chatsworth, just four years down the road!

## *The school of music*

With Edna and I teaching piano! That began one year before moving from Fannin to Gilmer County. I had 50 students and Edna 25, a total of 75! Each Monday and Tuesday was devoted to this venture as "teaching days!" The main focus remained in Fannin County while we lived in Gilmer and it continued for three years. The schools were *very cooperative* as we used their pianos and their heated buildings! I said to myself back then some 44 years ago, "Someday I'll return to these mountains and will listen to myself playing the piano through these students!" I spoke prophetically — as all speech is! We did return to the mountains and you can hear some of these students, now in their 50's, playing pianos in churches all over these mountains. That makes me feel real good! And, I am still alive to enjoy it! I must say it is hard to realize I have been involved in so many things! I needed to write this book for myself — if for no other! I can see myself sitting around reading it as I have plans to live until 124, forty-five more years!

Bojo was born while here in Gilmer County — our other boxer dog! He spent the next several years with us until he disappeared one day atop Fort Mountain. He grew up with our son, Michael, along with Snowball, our "spiritual cat!" You'll hear about Snowball later — and what a story I have to tell about him!

## *My doctorate*

That "came to me" while we were in Gilmer County! (A statement from quantum physics that I *have come* to understand!) But I also went after it! All the way to Louisville, Kentucky, while still living in Gilmer County!

What a fulfilling experience this was! It was a *crowning affirmation,* both of myself and my *roving ministry!* All my experiences seemed to *fit* into the scenario of my doctoral pursuit!

I had given up on any direction of a doctoral program until I heard that my alma mater, the Southern Baptist Theological Seminary had established a program for men like me. Mid-career pastors who would like to evaluate themselves and their ministries! This was just for me! I enrolled and the next two years I *soared like an eagle* educationally and theologically!

But first, how I "got in!" A group of us went to Louisville for our *orientation* — it was to see if we "qualified" for acceptance into the program. We were told that we must meet five of six *"qualification areas"* before we could even be considered for acceptance! I remember the statement of Dr. Harold Songer, "You'll have to have at least a score of 1100-1200 on your G.R.E. (Graduate Record Exam)." At that moment my heart "plunged" a little, as my G.R.E. was only 800! Or, so I thought! The truth was my record was much higher, as I had only counted half of it! For several years I had lived with this *mistake!* Living in falsehood, error — I was convinced of it!

I was exempt from the entrance exam, a comprehensive exam of my graduate seminary work. This was because my grade point average was a solid B+ to A–! Was I ever glad I had *been serious* at my studies earlier!

Dr. Songer concluded, "In about 30 days you will receive a letter from me. It will begin with 'Dear Mr. Poole, I am happy to inform you that *you have been accepted* into the Doctor of Ministry program, OR, I am sorry to inform you that, after careful review of your credentials, *you have not been accepted* into the program.'"

The day came and the letter arrived! I had been watching for it for days! The postman delivered it to the door. I reached for it, and *slowly* opened it! I allowed my eyes to glance at the opening paragraph: "Dear Mr. Poole ... I am happy ..." I read no more! I shouted! I had my degree! Although it was two years away, it was as good as if I were "walking across the stage!" I knew that if I were only accepted into the program I could do *anything* they required! Remember the "can do college work" after receiving the "A" in Greek back at Trevecca — twenty-two years earlier as a college freshman? Also, when I spoke to my mother in the front yard after the first quarter of college work back at Christmas 1948? A "sad" part of all this is that my mother passed just one month earlier than the letter!

The doctoral program was a blast! I breezed through! It was challenging, but easy! I had developed such good study habits that learning new material came quite easily to me. It was said that this was the "Harvard University of Baptists!" High standards and requirements! It didn't matter to me — I was having fun! Wow!

The name Clarence Drummond stands out from the two years at Louisville. We participated in the same carpool in riding from Dalton to Louisville. You can get pretty well acquainted when you spend eight hours in the front seat of a car! One day while passing through southern Kentucky, we passed a herd of cattle alongside one of those beautiful hills. I *very nonchalantly* said, "My Dad owns those cows!" Clarence told me later that he thought for a moment "what kind of *kook* is this?!" But the context of the moment was such that it *came across* as a *very real* statement! I explained to him that my Father — God — owned them, whom I referred to as "my Dad!" Somehow or other, a connection was established and we were joined together in spirit. Immediately we became *close friends,* and for the next three to four hours, Clarence "poured out his heart" to me about a *very intimate* matter, which he had never shared. Something he couldn't share with anyone else! Such camaraderie! It all happened in such a simplistic way. From a casual comment to the sharing of a profound experience — in which Clarence "experienced a freedom" he said he had never known! When we returned the next week, Clarence told me that was all he talked about the whole weekend! Including his sermon on Sunday at his Atlanta church! I find it *strangely beautiful* how such casual encounters turn out to be such *dynamic* relationships! There was such profound meaning in what occurred that day that would be a great topic of discussion in some graduate school of psychology. And it did not happen in a classroom but traveling down the highway!

## *The charismatics*

I "won my wings" with my colleagues one afternoon as I was chosen to share my problem with charismatics! We were asked to list *significant problems* we had experienced as pastor and I chose my encounters with charismatics. I was selected to be the first. I was glad because I wanted to get it over with! Was I ever surprised!

I sat in the middle of about forty of my *graduate peers* — highly successful pastors from across the nation! There I held sort of a press conference as I shared my story, then fielded questions. I will never forget when the accent of one word brought the house down. I related that the charismatics with whom I had dealt were so insistent with the way one pronounced "Holy Geohost!" Laughter ensued as I was in command of my audience and having fun! I will not share the essence of my encounter with "spirit filled holy Ghost freaks," except to say that from my vantage point, they had been negative and so it seemed from my peers! From my experience that day, with the accent of one word — I became sort of a hero and they thought I knew a lot in this area when I really didn't! I learned that their perception of me was probably as important (more so) than the real thing! The *whole thing* was funny to me for the next two years. I dealt with other events in a similar way! I discovered that *how* one deals with a matter is as valuable as the essence of what one shares. (I hope this makes a *little* sense to the reader.)

Graduation day came and I walked across the stage for the "fifth time" as all the others who had earned their doctorates stood! This was for me a day of affirmation! I was now Dr. Oscar Poole, A.B., M.R.E., B.D., M.Div., D.Min. Afterward while parading around out in the yard, in all our colorful regalia, Greg, our son, came up to me and shook my hand and said, "Congratulations, Dad!"

## *Added note to problem-solving*

Following sharing my encounter with charismatics — and since their perception was that I was a problem-solver, I was asked to sit in on other discussions my fellow doctoral candidates faced. It became my responsibility to analyze the basic dynamics of problem-situations and to give possible *options* to solving them! Me? A problem-solver? I guess it may be that much of my ministry had been involved in problems — I'm not sure *how many* of them I actually *solved!*

## *Meanwhile, back at the ranch*

The Gilmer parish, that is, in Georgia. While pursuing my doctorate at Louisville and serving as a *full-time* pastor of the Gilmer parish, I was able to give leadership to the building of a new church at Cartecay. You will find my name inscribed on the cornerstone with others even today as sort of a *lasting memento!*

Also it was my privilege to draw the architectural plans for the Nine Mile United Methodist Church that was constructed within three months after leaving as pastor. A new parsonage was built in Ellijay on a hill overlooking the city — all paid for upon entrance!

I was asked by Dr. H. Dan Rice, my beloved former district superintendent, to write a little booklet about the Gilmer experience. This I did, entitled "Miracle in the Mountains!" It was published and distributed throughout the North Georgia Annual Conference.

A further word about the "plans" I drew for the Nine-Mile Church. I drew the plans, the church took them to Pickens Tech. They copied them onto blue paper, thus we had blue prints! This literally happened!

So much took place while we served the churches in Gilmer County! I don't know who received the most, they or me! Little did I know we were "blazing new trails" for small churches! It is such a blessing to relive this story as I write this record of my *life's journey!* I feel affirmed *all over again!* It is a feeling I cannot describe!

It's time to move on! Or that's what the Methodist system said. Not I! I was happy doing my *thing!* Somehow, the horse and buggy mentality of Methodist preachers being moved about every three or four years still lingers! I have often wondered how much *creativity* has been lost by this old-fashioned, *worn-out* system! But, before we go, let me share the "baptism story!" I told this in my doctoral program and they loved it!

The year was 1973, the place Mountaintown Creek. I had seventeen persons to baptize! All requested the mode of immersion! Most people are not aware that the United Methodist Church allows all three modes: aspersion, affusion, or immersion (sprinkling, pouring or immersion). Most everyone knows what the latter is, as Baptists have placed that into the "national psyche!"

Seventy-five persons gathered down by the bridge where Mountaintown Creek crosses Highway 52. They were singing, "Shall We Gather at the River!"

But, where is the pastor?

I was "hiding in the woods!" At the proper moment I cried out, *"Repent, Repent! Bring forth fruit meet for repentance!"*

I came out of the woods reading, loudly and dramatically, when John the Baptist came out of his woods doing the same!

You will discover that Mountaintown Creek much resembles the Jordan River at Jerusalem where I also baptized ten others later!

This baptism story was *typical of the things we did* while serving the Gilmer parish.

It's time to go see the district superintendent about moving! It's an unwritten law that pastors are supposed to move up into larger, more affluent churches to establish their careers. As far as I was concerned, mine was already established and I was already *up*!

Just before leaving the house to drive to Dalton to see Dan Rice, I heard a voice, "Look into your Bible atop the dresser!" I obeyed what I *thought* I heard. With my eyes shut, I opened at random — my eyes fell on three words: "Some other place!"

I drove on to Dalton, and within three months, June of 1975, moved to Thomaston, Georgia, to assume leadership of the Hightower Memorial United Methodist Church! This time the move was made by others, my superiors in the church hierarchy, and we are moving *up*, so they said!

## Chapter XIII
## Thomaston, Georgia — 1975

The next two years, 1975-77, are fairly inconsequential. *Very little* happened, and the reason, to me, seemed *obvious.* I was appointed to the Thomaston, Georgia Hightower Memorial United Methodist Church. The "honeymoon" lasted three months. That means the newness of the new pastor soon wore off! The pastor's wife, Edna, could not cook *cuisine meals* for the women's groups, as did the former minister's wife!

Trivia! Typical in-fighting over matters that had no significance, except that many of the women held no desire but to keep matters stirred!

Hightower was a "mill" church! As any pastor in the North Georgia Conference knows, that is "enough said!" These were people whose jobs in the local cotton mill depended on "those folks on the other side of town — the First Church people!"

The people of the Hightower congregation felt themselves inferior to those elite people on the *west* side. A very prominent family had given the land and built the church building for them, something I feel is tragic! We were second-class citizens and no one *expected* us to do anything, so we didn't!

We "had" church alright. Visited patients in hospitals, a good thing, except when the minister missed one day, the whole town knew it!

The two years was a misfit! They did not need me and I did not need them! You've heard of Christ (in the old Apostle's Creed) about "descending" and "ascending" — well, the time spent at Hightower was for me, a *descending* experience!

About the only *exciting thing* during my two years at Hightower was when Greg shot the neighbor's dog! Our neighbor's dog, two blocks over, "invaded" Keith's chickens! He dug under the wire fence, killed several, and *maimed* what was left! He literally "tore the chickens apart!" So, Greg borrowed a friend's 12-gauge shotgun and let the dog have it! Responding in kind. The dog was *after* the last chickens when Greg fired the gun! I tried, as best I could, to patch up the ensuring neighborly relationship, paid the vet bill and let Greg know, "that's just something you do not do — the minister's son shooting the neighbor's dog!" It's a *good* thing the neighbor was not a member of our church! I actually think it was a *Baptist dog!*

I communicated with Dan Rice up in Dalton and told him to *get me out of here!* In June of 1977, I "ascended" to the pastoral leadership of the First United Methodist Church of Chatsworth, Georgia. This was just across the mountain from the Gilmer parish! At least I was "close by" to where the miracles had taken place!

# Chapter XIV
# Chatsworth — 1977-79

Back home again ... in North Georgia!

Chatsworth was a stately place. Not known for very much as it, too, was off to one side.

The previous pastor, known for his beautiful garden, left us some fresh asparagus that came up both years we were there! That's about as exciting as this chapter unfolds — except for the trip to the Holy Land when Edna and I took twelve persons "across the sea and baptized them in the Jordan River!"

## *One of the Bishop's favorites*

Strangely enough I had become one of the bishops favorites! I think it was because of the highly successful ministry in Gilmer County two years earlier and the fact that I am now "Dr. Poole!"

Edna and I found twelve people to go with us to the Holy Land (if you found ten, two could go free!). Off we went! Off to the wild blue yonder! Up and down those "hills of Galilee!"

The bishop was drawn to our group and we spent the week chumming with our bishop who had become chairman of the World Methodist Council! Wow! Big time *association*! Our bishop was a big cannon — that was his name! And we were getting to be *close buddies!*

Shortly before making the journey, the leader of the whole excursion of about 300, said — "Whatever you do, if you baptize anyone in the Jordan River, do not let the bishop know. He has a 'theological hang-up' about anyone getting re-baptized!"

You guessed it! My whole group wanted to be baptized in the Jordan River — by me! Sunday came and we all had some free time. My group and I rented two taxi's and "down to the River" we headed — a distance of about 65 miles. At the time, the government of Israel had not constructed public bath facilities for tourists to change clothes, so we prepared ourselves in our cars out in the parking lot! (I might add that I changed mine in between two cars!)

Baptize we did! One woman "came up shouting!" She was one of the Baptists who went along with us! I had two members of our team baptize me!

We are on our way back to Jerusalem to rejoin the bishop and others who had been "flocking" together. As we walked down the Kidron Valley the bishop said, "Dr. Poole, we missed you today! Where you been?" I replied, "Oh, we went sightseeing down the road toward Galilee!"

"Come on, now Oscar, tell him where you've been!" Hoyt Jenkins said aloud! I stepped back a step or two, put my finger over my mouth with a sign for Hoyt to shut up! He did not!

## Oscar Poole

"Come on, Oscar, tell the bishop where you been!" Somehow, word had gotten to the bishop and he already knew! Something I did not know!

My evasive comments ended when I somehow admitted, "We've been down to the Jordan River!" "What did you do there?" asked the bishop. "Oh, we baptized a few!" I have forgotten the series of statements that followed, except that there came over us a "silence" in our conversations for the next few minutes! I choked and we went on! (I thought to myself — I'm in for it now!)

We finished our trip to the Holy Land and returned home without incident.

The next week the Conference weekly newspaper came out with the bishop's editorial. He told the whole thing! All about "Dr. Poole baptizing twelve persons in the Jordan River!" He concluded by saying, "For years I have secretly wished I might be baptized in the River Jordan!"

Just think — I could have baptized the bishop! I missed it!

Even though I missed it on that one, there followed a great amount of publicity, all positive! It was a dramatic, happy, and almost romantic experience! What will I get into next?!

## *La Vie is born! 1978*

While we were living at Chatsworth in 1978, that is, the legal entity of La Vie!

For years I had yearned to have a spiritual retreat center — a secluded place in the woods — where God lives! I had increasingly — since camp meeting days at the old Nazarene Campground in Florida — experienced how God seemed so real in places like that!

Also, I had witnessed that often I could hardly find a trace of His presence in places called "church buildings!" Stained glass windows, pulpits and all the rest! Pews that actually cause physical back pain, artificial sounds, even organs and pianos. I preferred God's real house — the "out of doors" — the majestic mountains, the "wind blowing in the trees," the bubbling brooks, the whippoorwills, crows, oceans that *roared* and wind blowing in your face!" Like Julie Andrews, I had *been there* and never wanted to *come back!*

I have since learned that LIKE attracts LIKE (a phrase from the book "The Secret" and from quantum physics).

One day the phone rang out of the blue! "I want to give you the land for your retreat center!" One of the super big wows of my life! The lady, hardly known by me, had overheard my expressions for such a place when I had been at the Cartecay church a few years earlier.

## Oscar Poole

It was perfect! One hundred five acres of *the most beautiful mountain land!* It had a 40-acre lake in the front with great access from a paved road! The land was located out Roy Road over in Gilmer County.

"This is it!" The place of my dreams — FREE!

I prepared myself by obtaining a non-profit organization from the state of Georgia.

I visited the property on many occasions! The wind blew there! The crickets sang! I fell asleep under a tree! Visions of people gathering to enjoy God, his world and each other!

The day came to accept the clear deed. Just before driving over to Ellijay to accept this gift, the lady called. "Now, you know, I would want a *few restrictions.* I have inserted them as part of the deed-title!" Uh-oh! Warning! Trouble ahead! Restrictions for a "non-restricted" guy like me?

I accepted the gift and for the next seven days we owned 105 acres debt-free. But my heart was heavy! *This is not right!* At the close of the seven days I thanked her, but informed her I could never live with her *restrictions* and handed the deed back to her! That was a sad day, but also one of great relief!

The legal corporation of La Vie Ministries remained and would come into play years later! (That would be eight years, when the present 12-acres of pristine mountain land located at Mineral Bluff, Georgia, came as a gift, this time with no strings!

I'll discuss this down the road, when we get to it! We have some more "wilderness-wandering" to do!)

June 1979 came and it was "time to move again!" The last day of school came and I drove Michael to the high school — the Murray County High School — where he would graduate that evening. Edna and I were seated in the balcony looking down while "Pomp and Circumstance" was played. There's Michael, our last to leave the nest! It broke me up! It required a full year to get over this experience! Proud? Absolutely! But, sad? You had better believe it! Edna handled the matter *much better* than I! Just one of *life's traumas* to report, to which I know many reading this book can relate!

## *On the road again!*

Back to our house in New Smyrna Beach, where we would build that "dream church" — one like Robert Schuller's in Garden Grove, California — community, non-denominational, sophisticated, dealing with *relevant issues* — sort of like the "pot of gold *somewhere, somewhere ... over the rainbow!*" We were not following any yellow brick roads, but we were traveling over some very rough, broken ones!

During our stay back in New Smyrna Beach, we considered moving to Alabama to live near our son, Darvin. No real rationale, just more wandering! We did not follow this crazy hunch, although we did spend three months at the little town of Weaver, Alabama.

The year of 1979-80 was not a very good year! Depression was beginning to settle in! I had blown it! Tremendously successful, never satisfied! What was this restlessness within my breast? What's wrong with me? Do I have an emotional problem? These and other emotions plagued me as we managed to get through the year back home in our little house in New Smyrna Beach.

## *The Jim McDonald Story*

One of the bright spots of the year at NSB was that of "getting to know" Jim McDonald! This was truly a great event and one that Edna and I hold dear to this day! Jim and I did our morning walks each day. Jim served as a schoolbus driver with Wynelle Smith, my sister, for the Volusia County Schools.

Jim shared with me his deepest, most intimate feelings of his *encounters* with God! I'll never forget! It was a Friday. The day before he had attended mass at his Roman catholic church. While there, he had a vision!

There was a Holy Presence — ambiance surrounding us as we walked! I remember exactly the very place in the street — when Jim shared that during the celebration of the mass, he "looked up, saw Jesus in a statue ... Jesus came off that statue and came into me!"

You could tell this was for real! Jim HAD AN ENCOUNTER WITH GOD! It was quite different from my tradition, but so what? I received everything Jim said as a "living vital relationship with God!" It was moving!

Jim did not use the word "saved," rather he said, "I was blest!" The very next week he, Wynelle, Edna and I visited a Pentecostal church and we sang, "I am blest, I am blest, every day of my life I am blest!"

Am I BLEST to have Jim as my *close friend?* You can count on that!

This is one of those "hard to believe" stories that occur in each of our lives! I witnessed it almost first hand! In fact, I am the first person with whom Jim shared this! Even before his priest! And this was not a confession, but an affirmation!

Today Jim is the senior pastor of a large Roman catholic complex in Lima, Ohio. About three years ago, Edna and I stopped by to see Jim, as he was *that very week* moving into his parish! We slept in his bed even before he did!

Take a look at this greatest of experiences *right in the middle* of one of my worst years! How proud Edna and I are of Father Jim McDonald! We are "blest!"

## *1980*

Spring came! It always does! I had communicated with Methodist Church officials in Florida, and would you believe, they offered me a church! Unbelievable, yet true!

OSCAR POOLE

## *The Alturas United Methodist Church*

Here we are at the end of the world! Not really, just seemed so!

Nestled amongst beautiful orange groves was the city of Alturas, known for being the highest altitude in central Florida. A beautiful church building with stained glass windows where you "have church!" We "had church" — went through the motions, called "liturgy," for an hour per week. The rest of the time was spent "carrying out the trash" each Thursday morning. No challenge! Not much of *anything!* Just "Be!"

We did find Michael a job pruning orange trees. Trees that had been damaged from frosts that occasionally came that far south had to be pruned continuously. It was a hot, boring job, but that's what it was — a job! One day Michael encountered a wild fox. That evening he said to me, "Dad, did you ever see a fox trot?!" Also, the afternoon he arrived for his summer job in between semesters, Edna and I overheard him on the phone when he told his girlfriend, describing Alturas, "I've just seen this one part, the post office, a store, and five or six other buildings!" Little did he know that was the whole town!

None of the above statements are meant to detract from the natural beauty of the area. If you like orange grove country, you were right in the middle of it! The people were to be commended for their New England work ethic.

## There's Only One

One Sunday I invited Jim McDonald over to "give his testimony." This was before he left for several years of seminary. Jim often, when pronouncing his name, declared, "Not MAC, not MUC, but MC-Donald!"

That day I printed in the bulletin, which I had carefully concealed until the very start of the service, at the sermon title section: "Not MAC, not MUC, but MC-Donald!"

Jim looked over at Wynelle and whispered, "did you see what that fool had written in the bulletin?"

Well, you had to find *something* to stir up a little thing called *life!* We lived there six months.

The summer of 1981 ended and it was time to move on! Can you believe that during the summer the bishop from the North Carolina Conference of the United Methodist Church invited me to come to a little church in Fayetteville, North Carolina! Besides he offered me "full connection" (that's full status as an elder in that conference). That was the bishop that I could have baptized in the Jordan River! Have you ever heard such a story as I am trying to relate in this book? Will this ever *settle down?!*

As we were leaving town in early October 1981, I stopped the truck on the edge of town. I got out, left the engine running, took my shoes off, made sure some of that famous Florida sand was on the bottoms, "looked back" one last time toward the little village "left behind" and shook the sand off — put the *clean* shoes back on ... and left!

## Oscar Poole

This time with no dogs — although one "spiritual cat", Snowball — and no chickens! We have a 12-hour trip ahead of us, I driving the U-haul truck, Edna following in the family car! This was a sight America had seen, several times. We spent one night over in South Carolina. We woke up singing "Nothing could be finer than to be in Carolina in the morning!" Ate at a Waffle House, and on we went, up Interstate 95 and finally, crossed over at the famous Pedro's "South-of-the-Border" into what would surely become the *Promised Land!*

## *I "saw" a note*

As soon as we had crossed into North Carolina I had a vision! I "saw" *in my imagination* a hand-written note on the door where we'd be landing within one hour! Sure enough, upon arrival there was a note on the door! It read, "Do not move into the house. Call this number!"

I did! The lady came over and we talked. There had been trouble in River City! The Sunday before the church board met, "We do not want that concert grand piano in our church!" I had one in the truck! They preferred an old out of tune spinet! Does this reveal anything of the mentality I'm about to face in my new congregation? Just wanted the reader to know what kind of note we started out with in North Carolina!

I called the district superintendent! He said, "Unload the piano!" Can you imagine the tension we experienced the following Sunday — our first — when the congregation of 37 souls came out "to meet the new preacher?" I did not know much about the "giving off" frequencies — high and low — at that time, but I was about to learn!

You can read all about this subject in the book by David Hawkins, M.D., Ph.D., *Power Versus Force.* It's all there! But that day it was all *there*! Don't forget that I had *weathered* that County Fair fiasco years earlier, gaining a vital thing called *experience.*

"What a life," you say! So do I! In what is called "ministry" you can expect *most anything!* Expect or no, *troubled waters* are bound to come. Make sure you build a bridge before it *overflows* its banks! Especially is this true if you are an innovative and *avant garde* kind of leader!

## *The church flourished*

Within three months the congregation grew to a hundred, and then 200! And more! The budget increased from $17,000 to $100,000 — six times! We bussed in children from a poor area and gave them private tutoring on Tuesday afternoons. We bought five acres of land next door and began to fill it with cars, while the people went inside for worship. It was fun hiding out in the storage shed as I peeked through the crack in the door and saw people arriving that I had visited the week before!

Soon visions began to appear that we could become the largest United Methodist congregation on the whole east coast! We were half-way between New York and Florida along

I-95. All the "big" Methodist churches were in Texas! And, as I look back, we could have achieved it! What was there to stop us? Nothing, except *troubled charismatics and a threatened hierarchy!*

An amazing situation was emerging! A "coming together" of "spirit-filled," disgruntled *establishment* church officials! What I was learning is that organized religion is threatened by success! What? Whoever heard of such a thing? From a child I was always happy when the church became filled with people! It made God look good!

Let me quickly explain that it is the "old line" of "organized religion' that is threatened by success, not the *new brand* of "anything goes" of what I call "skip to my Lou" churches. This new wave of "hodge-podge" Christianity is not the *eclectic* nature of what I feel a part — although I am "connected" even to them, sometimes regrettably!

It is traditional Christianity that has been threatened when one appears with a "theology that works!" It has been "failure-oriented" emphasizing (wrongly in my belief system) the failure side of Christendom! The dying on the cross, agony, failure and the like! It stopped short of the resurrection which glories in new life, abundance, joy, thrill, blessing and success! I am sure some will read this and wonder what I am talking about. Let him who has true *spiritual discernment* understand! The church has been plagued with this failure disease all my life! The irony of the matter lies in the fact that the church has been dying on the vine — yet this should not be too difficult to understand as it received what it asked for!

(See my book *"Speak-To-It!"* in which I deal with "you get what you think and say!") It is very obvious to me that we should "expect" death when death is one's focus. I guess this phenomenon is overlooked by many, when it blatantly stares us in the face! It's like when one cannot see the forest for the trees!

Count me out of the *old* and into the *new!*

There is a NEW WIND blowing! It's from the grassroots up! It is NON-CHURCH! It is NON-RELIGIOUS! It is SPIRITUAL!

It is "beyond charismania!" I preached this message at Fayetteville and you should have seen the charismatics run! The ones who did not run stayed and fought! They, like all the rest of history, wanted to *rope off boundaries* and stake their claims on some newfound religious experience — declaring that what they had experienced was a final revelation from God! That they "had it all!" Their newness became old! They fought the next round of any new revelation — so on it goes! A new revelation wears off! A new one appears! The tragedy is that each generation is left standing somewhere with old stagnant truth that once "glowed in the twilight" — now old, while God has left the station (a train metaphor) and has ascended to new heights!

## *New move and it is glorious!*

There is a "new move" of the Spirit! The winds are FRESH! EVERYTHING is NEW! It is BEAUTIFUL! It's a NEW WAVE OF HISTORY!

## Oscar Poole

IF IT'S NOW, IT'S NEW! IF IT'S NEW, IT'S NOW! IT'S NEVER BEEN DONE BEFORE! There are *no past models!* We have entered *uncharted waters!* We are moving into a NEW DIRECTION that this NEW WIND IS TAKING US! It's EXCITING! It's CHALLENGING! It's NEW! NEVER BEEN DONE BEFORE! It's NOW!

We are depending upon the VOICE INSIDE! We are LISTENING! HEARING! RESPONDING! The ESSENCE (love) is the same — changes not, but the forms are totally *different!* Expressions of a *new theology are beginning to abound!*

This NEW MOVE is greater than anything in the PAST! Even Pentecost (Acts 2) and all the REFORMATIONS *combined!*

I suppose the above was *birthing* within me during my three-year Fayetteville experience. The "old" gave way to the 'new!" AND AM I GLAD! That's the reason for all the above CAPITAL letters! And EXCLAMATION POINTS! Truly *exciting!*

It is a THRILL to BE ALIVE during a time like this! The problems are CRUCIAL! The stakes are HIGH! Terrorist threats and SURVIVAL itself, but GREATER THAN THESE IS THE "YET-TO-COME" TRUTH that SETS US FREE! HALLELUJAH! Beginning to sound like camp meeting! Even GREATER than "back in those good old days at the old Nazarene Campground!" Hallelujah! AMEN! "To God be the GLORY! Great things He (in us and sometimes AS us) is doing!" (I expect to hear about these comments just written at Glen and Frieda Bowen's beautiful farm down here in Gardiner, Florida,

- 165 -

as I am writing these few pages early this morning out in our motor home!)

I am leaving out the low frequency stuff that occurred at Fayetteville. While I was a threat to the "establishment" I too was threatened! I think I bottomed out in my spirit!

## *Snowball*

Oh, the cat experience! Snowball, our beloved white SPIRITUAL CAT! If you want a *great cat story,* here is one! Snowball rests *under a rock* at La Vie, our mountain retreat center located near Blue Ridge, Georgia.

What a cat! Snowball!

At 5 a.m. one morning I found myself in the backyard of our Fayetteville home — PROSTRATE — on the floor of our little storage shed. Face-down, my spirit cried, "WHY, LORD? WHY?" I forgot to ask "WHAT!" My perspective certainly was not clear! I did not realize that *what was going on* was God-orchestrated!

The night before I passed by the home of one of our church members, hosting an *unofficial committee* to get rid of the pastor — me! I was the AGENDA! Unless you have been there you cannot *resonate* with my feeling! People who had joined the church under my leadership (all five of them) turned on me! They were discussing and taking *notes,* later handed over to the bishop who had traveled with Edna and me in the Holy

Land — the one I *almost* baptized! Strange story, you say? Agreed! I am going to save most of the Fayetteville story until a later date. It deserves a full book! It is so full of low frequencies that I do not wish to lower mine at this time! It must serve a redemptive, positive HIGHER FREQUENCY than the story itself! That may happen. It would be an "exposé" on organized religion, but since it has exposed itself why should I add to it?

Back to Snowball — our spiritual cat!

It's five a.m. Here I lay, giving birth to my personalized meditations, which has become one of my best contributions to others who may follow me — Affirmations of Faith! (See my first book, *"Speak-To-It!"* that came later as a result of these birth pangs lying on the floor in the tool shed!).

I said, aloud, I am the *only person* listening. Quietly. Muttering. "I am far from oppression and fear does not come nigh me!" I repeated it. Again. Each time I said it, *something* way down on the inside responded! It felt good! Strengthening. I can't explain!

While on the floor, enjoying something going on with God, Snowball enters the building! He climbs up on my back and begins to purrrr! He *pushes* with this front paws as if to say, "Yes, Oscar, pray on!" The feel of the warmth of God's love on my back! I am AFFIRMED! I AM BLEST! God is with me! Not the camaraderie of a supportive friend, but of our family pet, Snowball! Did you know you can "experience God" through a cat? I suppose cats can be spiritual too, as Box, our other family pet, in the giving of his life in an act of love!

We're about to leave Fayetteville. Defeated, discouraged, we're "on the road again!"

A brief analysis of the three years at Fayetteville: I'm sure you've heard of "being so low, you had to reach up to touch bottom!" That's where I was! This became my DARK NIGHT OF THE SOUL! It seems that every great man has experienced this! I'm not saying that I am great — although greatness lives inside me! But I am saying that I went through a "hell of an experience!" No one should have to endure such an *emotional disaster!* But it was good for me! What THEY meant for evil turned out to be the GREATEST of my life! Had I known this it would have *comforted* me — along with the cat! I know these statements sound goofy!

This dark night lasted for the next four or five years! But COME OUT I did! It was a process of pain that was *very difficult* to endure.

Now that the Fayetteville thing is in the PAST — almost forgotten — I am very thankful for the darkness. Now the "light shines brightly!"

Let me explain.

I think one has to plunge so low that he "finds himself!" That's what happened to me! I got in touch with myself! I found out who I really am! It was like a *clinic!* Very "primal!"

## OSCAR POOLE

The *greatest* benefit of the next few years was that I experienced the live mercy and grace of God! It became a *God and me* thing! I felt I was *stripped* of everything — even life itself! I thought I would never preach again, nor counsel a grieved person, nor "care for the dying!" Was I WRONG! You see, my THOUGHTS were in error! When my THOUGHTS changed, by an act of my will, I experienced a METAMORPHOSIS from a "lowly worm" to a "butterfly" — only now I am FLYING HIGH like an eagle!

This CHANGE did not happen overnight! There was some more *pain* and lonely days! Occasionally even now, I fall off the wagon — but not often.

Suffice it to say that while in darkness, feeling *alone* and in much despair, I BEGAN TO SEE THE LIGHT! Ever so dimly! But there it was! I TREMBLE for joy THIS MOMENT (NOW) as I reflect on it! Words fail me to describe it! I only hope the *essence* of it comes through! HOPE, hope to get more out of this dungeon! I am inside what John Bunyan called the "SLOUGH OF DESPOND!" There must be some kind of degree for this learning, as I graduated SUMMA CUM LAUDE!

I NEEDED this! I had to DIE to AWAKEN! Though I had the "world by the tail on the downhill pull!" Was ON TOP — "Minister of the Year" (three times), "One of one hundred most CREATIVE ministries" — LOST it! Not really! You can NEVER LOSE who you ARE! I ONLY THOUGHT I HAD! It's STILL THERE! It's ME! Wow! If you should experience something like this, you should hear "Weeping may endure for a night, but

## There's Only One

JOY COMES IN THE MORNING!" Hallelujah! AMEN! Sing praises to the Lord! It's AMAZING what I learned while down! I probably would never know what feeling good is all about had I not gone through the agony of defeat! I think now that I recommend such an experience — there is nothing like being REBORN during mid-life!

Can you begin to see why I HATE religion with such passion? It was the religious people who did this to me! They were faithful churchgoers! They even thought they were doing God service! By the way, it was the same mentality that "sent Jesus to the cross." But, I love them! They are some of my best friends!

One of the complaints brought against me was that I had often said that what we were doing was "avant garde" to which I plead "GUILTY!" Exactly right! We are on the cutting edge of a whole new movement!

To sum up the three years at Fayetteville, 1981-84, the WORST became my BEST! As I write this I FEEL SO GOOD about it! It was necessary! This is hard for me to believe, what I am telling you! But it is true — and glorious!

I think I may write about the Fayetteville fiasco — I may not — it is full of low frequencies and the very repeating of them pulls one down! Although I think now that I am beyond that as I see in a different light. (Can you believe, just as I wrote this sentence the sun came up! *Divine synchronicity?* And over a lake at that! Down here at South Bay, Florida, spending the day with my lovely wife, Edna in our motor home!)

Note: The reader will better understand many of the comments just mentioned as this book unfolds — it's like *progressive revelation* — one of the key parts of my theology. You can say that in these last few pages I have gone to preaching (pontificating)! This is my theology! I am writing it! But before I wrote it, I LIVED it! And besides, as I have put this on paper, I have experienced a new catharsis, just by telling it!

Oscar and Paul Coverdell

THERE'S ONLY ONE

Ariel View of Oscar Poole's Georgia Bar-B-Q

Republic National Convention; New York 2004

## Chapter XIV
## Charleston, West Virginia

The year is 1984. I am 54 years of age! We have 24 more years to go — we are two thirds through.

We moved to Charleston, Edna's hometown. No chickens! No dogs! Just one cat, Snowball. He's still with us! Where else were we to go? We did have a *little money* from the sale of our house and we owned sixty-five acres of land at Amma, West Virginia, 35 miles outside Charleston, reserved for the mountain retreat, La Vie! But this was not to be! Not there yet!

There is not much to report from Charleston. We are still in the wilderness! You know they call that state "Wild, Wonderful West Virginia!" We stayed there one year. Bits and pieces to report, but mostly sitting on the front porch, visiting with my mother-in-law — the one who said Edna and I would NEVER MAKE IT! Just thought I'd *throw that in!* We actually became friends! Maybe that's the reason for being at Charleston that year. I can't think of any other benefit. One year to get to know and love your mother-in-law!

That was the front porch of our mobile home atop one of those West Virginia hills overlooking a large valley near Elkview. We had purchased a small mobile home park, which was a *mistake!* In fact during the next five years of turbulence, not knowing where to go or what do to, I made several mistakes. It was a time of restlessness. I was like the "do nothing" congress that Harry Truman described many years earlier!

In beautiful West Virginia but not able to enjoy it! I had managed to buy a small farm, sixty-five acres not far from the trailer park, that I thought would become home to La Vie, the retreat center for which my spirit had longed! It seemed right, but it wasn't. It had not been the result of hearing that inner voice — it was solely the result of my *intellectual understanding* — big difference! You can *see* something in your mind — it can even be a good or great idea, but not be your true direction!

## *Another false direction*

One day my friend of 35 years, Tom May called and felt that "God had spoken to him," that I was the man to *follow him* in his great community church over in Lexington, Kentucky! (The following discussion "I told you NO!" is taken out of my book, *"God In The Marketplace".*)

## *"I Told You NO!"*

And, am I glad He did! I heard God, in a voice deep within my being, speak in a loud voice, clearly, unmistakably... "I TOLD YOU NO — DON'T YOU EVEN OPEN YOUR MOUTH!"

This is to encourage all of you who have been discouraged at "NO" answers. Allow me to put this in perspective.

## Oscar Poole

The place was in Kentucky, the time was 1986. The exact location was on Interstate 64 — just outside Lexington.

Edna and I were living near Charleston, West Virginia. I had been out of a church as pastor for a year. That was back when I still thought "ministry" was inside a specially-designed building with pews, pulpits and all that "stuff!"

T.T. May had been my dear trusted friend for 34 years. Tom was pastor of a non-denominational community church in Lexington and he wanted to retire. But there was a problem: Who do you get to follow you? Tom was trying to choose me, which was an honor, and I was trying to choose him — that is to become Tom's associate and then pastor.

It was a good, even GREAT idea! It offered about everything I had dreamed of. Association with long-time friends within a university city. I could see a far-reaching T.V. ministry! I could envision being near two of my alma maters — Asbury Seminary and Southern Seminary in Louisville. By now I had my doctorate, I was *somebody*. I wanted to accept Tom's gracious offer and get back into the flow of things! Especially after Tom said to me, "God told me you are the man!" I was excited! I couldn't wait!

Well, God had not "told" me! And even though it appeared to be the right thing to do I was struggling with accepting his offer. Tom saw that and suggested, "Oscar, why don't you take six weeks — come over here on the weekends and see if you get the feel for it. Then decide. You can do whatever you want ... preach, pray, sing, play the piano."

# There's Only One

So, for the next six weeks we did just that! Some weekends I would be high on the idea — the next my spirit would drag. Somehow in the pit of my stomach, it did not *feel* right. Sometimes there would be a tightness in my lower stomach. My spirit was trying to tell me, "This is not right!"

At the close of the six weeks — on Easter Sunday, 1986 — I had to give Tom an answer. I'll never forget the emotional moment when I told him, "Tom, I am honored that you have considered me to be associated with you in this church!" With tears in my eyes, I said, "Tom, we can't accept it." He replied, "Oscar, I knew you were going to say that."

A relief came over me and off we drove — back to a little trailer park we had purchased in West Virginia, some four hours away.

Monday came. I had one of those famous "Monday morning quarterback" sessions with Edna. I said to her, "Who are we to be turning down an offer from anybody? We don't have anything (speaking of an active, ministerial career) and I am saying 'no'? We could accept the offer temporarily and then when something else comes along we could accept that. This thing is so crucial (besides that we were going broke financially), that it's worth another 24 hours. Why don't I call Tom and go back one more time — today — just to see if we missed it!" She agreed. So I called Tom and headed back to Lexington.

## Oscar Poole

Just before reaching the city, I heard a voice, "I TOLD YOU NO — DON'T YOU EVEN OPEN YOUR MOUTH!" Clear, distinct, loud (all within my being — no "outside" voices!) Who was it? It was God! At least we were on speaking terms and I took comfort in that!

I arrived at Tom's house and after a few moments of general conversation, we went out to eat — would you believe, at a BAR-B-Q restaurant?

I hope you see the irony of this as our final life's dream was not far away as we were "led" into one of the most successful restaurant ventures in the nation — what is today "Col. Poole's Georgia BAR-B-Q, Inc.!"

We visited and spent the night with Tom and Bertha — then left the next morning and never said a word about going to work with Tom in the church! I have often wondered what Tom thought about that brief return trip! Maybe he thought I was crazy, or whatever. It had to seem strange. Tom has since passed away and I may never know what he thought!

What do you do when "you're not there yet?!" You KEEP ON MOVING (that is, if you are receiving a *true direction* from the *inner voice* INSIDE you in cooperation with the friendly universe that is always there to assist you! God, et. al., — ascended masters and others (there is a HEAVENLY HOST who work "together with God" who ALREADY know when and what you should do!). In fact, this was going on all the time but I did not know it! That expression about "hindsight is *so true!*

One learns a lot when he gets my age — 79! Again, if he learns to LISTEN — which you are about to observe, I did!

One great thing I have learned from my pilgrimage on this "space-ship earth" is that the "NO" replies from God are as important as the "YES" responses!

Oscar's "Piglet" in the Fourth of July Parade

## Chapter XV
## The Next Three Years

### *Are we there yet? Almost! 1986-89*
#### (Prelude in C Minor)

We're getting ready" for the GREATEST time period of my 79 years! (Just thought I'd use the above "C Minor" to remind myself at least that the living of these days is like "playing the piano" — practice and more practice! This is what I call pontificating, but O'Reilly calls it obliviating!)

### *Guidance comes!*

"I want you to return to Georgia!"

I have left Tom's house and I am headed home to Charleston with Edna waiting for me. I had not even discussed the matter with Tom — case closed!

I am bouncing along Highway 64 near Winchester, Kentucky, in our nearly worn-out white Chevette. My spirit is settled. I am relaxed.

When all of a sudden — out of the blue — that voice returned! This time it was not loud — but that "still, small voice" you read about in 1 Kings 19! It was casual. It was conversational.

### There's Only One

The voice spoke. Then I spoke. Now, here's a man "hearing a voice" and no one is in the car with him! It is God! Who else?

He said to me, "Where, after all these years, did I bless you the most?"

I thought for a moment. "In the mountains of north Georgia!" I said.

"Where were you the happiest and most content?"

I replied, "In the mountains of north Georgia!"

"Where did you prosper the most in all the years of your ministry?"

I said, "In the mountains of north Georgia!"

"Where did your family call home?"

"In the mountains of north Georgia!"

This was almost getting boring, repetitive, redundant — "In the mountains of north Georgia!" But I see now that He (God) was pulling it out of me and causing me to say the very answer to the culmination of my life's pursuit — *the mountains of north Georgia!*"

Then came that loud voice again, the one I had heard the day before — almost at the same place on the same highway — "I

OSCAR POOLE

WANT YOU TO RETURN TO THE MOUNTAINS OF NORTH GEORGIA!"

I almost shouted! Relief! I had found the answer to my quest — I had HEARD from God! He had, in the very midst of my confusion, spoken.

I could not wait to get back to tell Edna the good news!

I arrived at our mobile home in West Virginia.

"Edna," I said, almost embarrassingly, but with great joy and relief. "Guess where we are going?"

She stared and waited.

"BACK TO THE MOUNTAINS OF NORTH GEORGIA!"

Within three months we moved to "the mountains of north Georgia!" But even when we got there it took some "doings" to finally arrive at the destination, which eventually became world-renowned — the BAR-B-Q forum — notice I said "forum" — a newer and very different pulpit for ministry!

*Divine synchronicity* appears! That is, many things are converging to work together for our good!

Now that I've "heard from God," things begin to work toward that end! There is *great* theology here: Get your Divine signal first (that makes for a current theology), then you can expect *divine forces* to operate on your behalf!

We sold the trailer park. Also sold the 65 acres. That was very sad, but like the 105 acres earlier, I had to give it up! This for me was faith! Deep inside, I felt very good — at ease, peaceful, with some kind of inner knowing that I was doing the right thing! But how do you know you're doing the right thing when your life's record seems to indicate many wrong decisions and turns?

I can only say in the words of Tiny Tim, "You just know it!"

## *The truck is loaded (and so is the cat)*

We're off to see the wizard — the wonderful wizard of OZ-CAR! (He's not there yet, but when we get there, he will be!) There is a small yellow brick road in front of Col. Poole's BAR-B-Q today which says (arrow pointing), "To see the wizard of OZ-CAR!" How did he *get so wise?* This book reveals how!

We had just crossed over from the wild country of West Virginia, and stopped at a gas station in Grayson, Kentucky, when I told someone, "We just got the *heaven* out of West Virginia!" You see, when we move we IMPROVE both places — where we moved from and where we're going!'

We arrive! Earlier we had made a preliminary trip down to Georgia and bought a little "bamboo church" for $20,000 on a borrowed note co-signed by my friend, Dr. Jim Haymore, who had pledged he would help me.

Can you believe there was a cute little brick home right in the neighborhood of the little church? Jim, my beloved friend who assisted me nearly every step of the way, owned it and allowed us to live in it RENT FREE for the next two years!

## *The bamboo church*

A classic! The people who built it cut dried bamboo in half with a rip saw and nailed them all over the walls, including an altar, and finished them with shining varnish. It was beautiful! It was simple! It was unique! There probably was not one like it in the world. The bamboo was free! Oh, how I wish we still had this *precious* piece of architecture. It was an offering of *ingenious* mountain people who loved their God and *expressed* it this way! Far more saintly than the *more expensive* ones!

We began conducting services in the quaint building. Soon it was nearly full!

I'll never forget one Sunday, July 4, 1977, when a very sophisticated lady from Blairsville shouted when we sang the National Anthem! It was spontaneous! She was from Germany and had been raised under Hitler and did not take her freedom for granted! What moments of inspiration and celebration followed! Precious memories!

OH-OH! A few disgruntled charismatics showed up. They nearly always do! They love the spirit — especially the *spirit of control!*

There was one episode I'll never forget! It was full of positives, negatives and pure *Tom foolery!* It began when Pete Getta, an anointed man of God, gave a prophecy, which is proving to be true regarding this writer, followed by three days of turmoil that threatened to upset the cart, but turned out to be a tempest in a teapot when the three men left the church. The good thing was that their auras (frequencies) no longer were around to disturb the **PRESENCE** that was in that place! I can hear us singing 'Surely the Presence of the Lord is in this place...' — a powerful little chorus that everybody can sing, both liberals and conservatives — and even fundamentalists!

We visited around in other churches and got to listen to pianists who had learned their skills under our tutelage! That was thrilling in itself!

## *"They've got my idea!"*

I shouted as I saw the little BAR-B-Q rig, eight feet by twelve feet on wheels! We went right to it, bought a BAR-B-Q sandwich, and purchased it! The 8' x 12' rig, that is! Of course, there was a time-lapse of a few days.

We started selling BAR-B-Q! Didn't sell much because no one would buy it! Discouraged, broke, in debt, we sold it to a man who moved it to Blairsville, where he went broke and left it standing there. We had to go get it. Why? Because I held the mortgage on it — $35,000 worth! We hauled it to Tom Boyd's farm in Blue Ridge where it sat, alone, for nearly a year. We were out of business, out of hope, out of money — destitute!

## Oscar Poole

One morning I was watching a "Christian" television program. The spirit in me said, "That's ... (name left out because he is well-known). I went to see him. This well-known preacher informed me that declaring bankruptcy was the best course of action for me. I now have clearance to erase all debts and hit the road for God! (A thing I was good at, but not the "for God" part!)

We had no income, but we did have friends! They sent us cash offerings for months! One lady, Polly Benson from Texas, sent us $100 per month for four years! So did our son, Keith! What would we have done without them? They were there when we needed them — God's provision! Glen and Frieda Bowen were among these God-providers.

We sat one Sunday at the table in our little cabin — Tom, Naomi, Edna and I. I said, "Unless God acts sovereignly by next Friday, I will have to declare bankruptcy." Declare it? We already were that — bankrupt! After all, I have been "cleared" by one of our nation's spiritual leaders. It's okay! I'll never forget what Naomi said, quite casually, "It will be interesting to see how God works this thing out!"

Friday came. I went to see the bankruptcy lawyer in Marietta, Georgia. I said, "I'm here to declare bankruptcy! I want you to start the process!" He heard my story.

Then he looked straight into my eyes! "Get out of here, you're not ready to declare bankruptcy! Go home! Get that out of your mind!"

I headed home. Then God spoke! "He's right! We'll find a way out of this mess!"

Two-thirds vote: Two to one! A lawyer, God and a preacher! Who was right? Who do you think?

A wave of peace came over me! I knew it would be alright.

## The Wendell Cross story

During the two years leading up to the BAR-B-Q story, I met and tutored Wendell Cross, who lived one mile from La Vie. Wendell could not read. He was in his sixties! A country mountain man, a genius, but with no formal education!

Here is a little of the story. Wendell Cross owned and operated a gas station at Mineral Bluff. One day I came by, headed home to the Haymore house. My truck was about out of gas, and I had no money in my pocket.

I pulled in to the station. "May I have $5 worth of gas — on credit?" "Yes," his son replied, as Wendell was not there.

A couple of weeks later I was over at Blue Ridge, 5 miles to the south, when I heard that now familiar voice inside, "Don't buy gas at the Amoco station. Fill up at the Cross station in Mineral Bluff — after all, you owe them $5!"

Hear me, Fundamentalists! These words were from GOD! Therefore it was God's Word! Do you see — just as much as John 3:16. Not as important, but still words from God! I don't know of any place in the Bible where I could go to receive guidance on where to buy gas that day! Instead, it was direct communication from God, within my spirit! No question! This is what I heard and this is what I did!

I entered the station. There was Wendell Cross, the proprietor/owner. I carried on my usual foolishness. In fact, I was happy and free in my spirit and was singing a happy tune! Wendell shared with me that he had just come from the "tater patch" when he had been praying, "Lord, send me a teacher, so I can read!" Wendell knew the alphabet and could make out road signs and could tell where the men's restroom was, because "MEN" had three letters and "WOMEN" had five! Once he found "GENTS" and "LADIES" and that threw him. He had to ask someone standing in front of the men's room, "Do you know *which one* of these rooms is the men's?" "You're standing in front of it, you fool!" Wendell replied, "I knew it all the time, I just wanted to see if you knew where it was!"

*Divine synchronicity!*

Here's what Wendell shared with me that day about his prayer to "send me a teacher."

Wendell, too, heard a voice! "Go to the station!" That's all he heard. He thought something might be wrong! As soon as he said these words to me I replied, "I'm the teacher!" Why would I say that?

For the next two years I taught Wendell to read! Phonetically. "PER-simmon tree — not SIMMON tree!" Pre-fixes, fun songs about the alphabet, syllables, vowels (we never discussed diphthongs!). Slowly, Wendell began to sound out sentences! What a thrill it was when Wendell read the Christmas story from Luke 2 at a candlelight service the next Christmas Eve at the Bamboo Church!

I must say that while I am writing this story I can almost feel the tears coming down my cheeks as they did that Christmas Eve!

Teaching Wendell to read was one of the greatest thrills of my life! Columbus discovered America — or so they say — but I discovered Wendell Cross! For two years I tutored Wendell. Sometimes our lessons were in the dirt — North Georgia red clay dirt — sometimes on cardboard. Wendell was an eager learner! What a privilege for me! After our two years together I got Wendell into a literacy school where he excelled and received the highest honor in adult literacy education for the whole state of Georgia and spoke before an audience of 3,000 at the prestigious Jekyll Island in South Georgia!

To cap it all off, on Christmas Day, 1998, Wendell was featured on the *Today Show*. I appeared with him, only this time I was in the background! Can you believe that? Was I ever touched when Matt Lauer said, "Merry Christmas, Mr. Cross!" By the way, that's national T.V., NBC-TV! Did we attract that?!

Oscar Poole

## *La Vie returns!*

"Jarrell is going to give you that land for your retreat!"

This chapter backs up a bit from the above discussion. The time was shortly before the BAR-B-Q saga began, in 1988 when we were living in Mineral Bluff, Ga.

Where La Vie, our mountain retreat, now stands, a converted barn with a rock fireplace, a mountain stream, a meadow, a place to park motorhomes, and room for a new lodge — you know, that place where God seems to talk that I mentioned earlier?

I shall never forget the day that God spoke to me about Jarrell giving 12 1/2 acres of beautiful mountain land to us! It was a Monday morning at 7 a.m. when Jarrell Anderson called. Jarrell and his wife, Mary, were developing one hundred acres of land for homesites near Mineral Bluff on Piney Mountain. In his slow, deep voice, he said, "Oscar, I want to talk with you!"

I asked myself what I had done wrong... Isn't it strange that many of our responses to even good things are framed in some sort of a negative manner?

I told Jarrell that I was leaving immediately for the dentist's office over in Chatsworth to have a root canal, and I'd had a severe toothache all weekend.

## There's Only One

"Well," said Jarrell, "How about meeting Mary and me at the Fannin Inn for lunch upon your return?"

"Okay." I said. "Is 11 o'clock alright?"

"Yes," he said. "Mary and I will meet you at the Fannin Inn at 11 o'clock!"

I was puzzled. What did Jarrell want with me? Why is he bringing Mary with him and why did he ask that I bring Edna along? These and other thoughts ran through my mind.

Just outside Ellijay, on Hwy. 282, between Ellijay and Chatsworth, God spoke! (When God speaks, it's hard to forget the time and place!) That inner voice — loud, distinct, clear — out of the blue... "Jarrell wants to give you that land for the retreat!" That's exactly what I heard.

"Oh, no," I replied. "He's not going to do that!" (Notice my negative response!) Maybe I was shocked in disbelief — it's one of those too good to be true deals!

God's reply, "Yes, he is. He's going to give you that land!"

"Aw, no, he's not!" Here I go again with my great faith, a "man of the cloth," a minister, one who preaches faith — I can't believe what I am hearing!

So I went to Chatsworth and all the while the dentist is working on my tooth this matter is on my mind!

## Oscar Poole

A couple of hours later, now 10 a.m., I am returning home on the same highway and almost at the same place I heard God's voice again! "Yes, Jarrell is going to give you that land!" This time, the third time, I did not reply. I was beginning to believe that what I had heard *might* be true!

So, we all, Edna, Mary, Jarrell and I, met at the Fannin Inn, ate a nice lunch, had a pleasant conversation and left for our home back out toward Mineral Bluff — not a word about any land being given. We had never discussed a single time about having a retreat on the property, although I'm sure he had heard me talk about having a retreat center.

We drove into the front yard, Edna and I, in our white Chevette and Jarrell and Mary in his black Bronco. We all got out and gathered around the front hood of his Bronco. Jarrell reached for a large, rolled up document, opened it to the survey page of the property and said, "Mary and I want to give you the property for your retreat!"

Do you have any idea of how I must have felt? Well, I should not have been surprised — God had told me three times!

Does God speak today?! You tell me!

THERE'S ONLY ONE

The 'Shack'- Birthplace of Col. Poole's Georgia Bar-B-Q

The sign known from Georgia to Washington D.C.

Oscar Poole

# Chapter XVI
# The Promised Land
## *(Col. Poole's Georgia BAR-B-Q, Inc.)*

We're "getting there!"

The next twenty years *unfold one of the greatest sagas* of my life. Finding *fulfillment* through a BAR-B-Q shack!

"If you get on the side of that hill and do the menial work, I'll show the world what I will do!"

That inner voice!

A few pages back I mentioned about looking for a place to set up our 8' x 12' BAR-B-Q business.

Edna and I looked over the area. Somehow we felt an *inner urge* to look for a place 15 miles away in Ellijay, Ga., where our successful church ministry took place years earlier. While scanning for possible sights we noticed that trucks were digging out the mountain in the heart of East Ellijay on Highway 515 — the "Zell Miller Parkway" — the main four-lane thoroughfare built in recent years.

We were *drawn* to it. Began to ask questions. No one had any plans for it. They were moving the dirt off the mountain and dumping it into a hole across the street between the service road and the main highway.

What were they *really* doing? Preparing the new location for what has now become a north Georgia landmark and legend! The dirt placed in the ditch across the street became a paved parking lot (40 cars) for a "Park & Ride" area for the public to park their cars and carpool to and from their jobs toward Atlanta. But it was empty on weekends — that is, until Poole's BAR-B-Q began to explode and the lot filled up with customers! A quarter-million dollar parking lot — not even for the asking.

We rented the side of the hill for $100 per month. Borrowed more money and went to work selling BAR-B-Q! The first days' receipts were $208, and half of that was profit!

The real story that unfolded since is that of a rags-to-riches story, sort of a Cinderella one! Sometimes as I look back, I'm not even sure it's real.

## *The Voice*

While considering the hillside, fast being emptied of dirt, God spoke again! Precisely in these exact words, "If you get on the side of that hill and do the menial work, I'll show the world what I will do!" (I mentioned this one page back.)

## Oscar Poole

Am I glad that my spiritual growth and new understandings of how God works was operative and, am I glad that not only did I believe that God speaks today, but am I glad I *heard* Him!

And, the "menial" work we did! Edna and I worked 12 hours a day, seven days per week. The two of us spent 168 man hours per week! We did the work of four! We sold BAR-B-Q! Two and three hundred dollars worth per day! This was *big* for us!

People laughed at us! The place was tacky, so tacky it was "classic." We added a room — a 10' x 10' porch where we could watch T.V. between customers. The business grew to three and four hundred dollars per day, and we hired a part-time helper. Edna and I were able to "take off" a half day now and then. One day a customer arrived and found our helper asleep on the porch while he was watching T.V. She had to wake him up! "Sir, could you serve me some BAR-B-Q?!"

Here is a funny one! We decided we should sell French fries. So, we got a fry daddy, big enough to fry one small order at a time. It was right out on the front where everyone could see it! Three men were in line awaiting their orders. I'll never forget — Ermel Forrester — as he waited — his French fries cooking! He told me later that he said to another man in line, "I like that old boy! He has pretty good BAR-B-Q, but he'll never make it!"

Every time I see him I remind him of what he said!

## There's Only One

Oh — the room we added had a roof from off a chicken house. Literally! We placed two card tables for inside seating. We put plastic around the sides to keep the rain out.

It was "tacky." We built a small storage room outside for supplies — even placed a toilet and a sink in it. Then we added another room, this one with materials Fred Bailey gave me from tearing down a room he had added to a mobile home on his property. As a lasting memorial you can still see the name "Fred Bailey" on a plaque on the front door!

I must mention about the birth of the pigs scattered around which became the "seen around the world" PIG-HILL-OF-FAME!

The day before we opened I noticed we needed a new "Open-Close" sign. I thought, I'll go down to the feed store. They'll have a picture of a pig on a feed sack. I'll copy it and make a cute little sign." So I went to Carl Hill's local feed store and wound up with a pig-image (the Oscar Poole version) and solved the problem!

But now I had a new problem — I had some plywood left over! So I made about six more and stuck them around with mine and Edna's, plus Mark, Carl, Fred, Bob and Melissa's names on them. This was done very timidly, as I thought they might hit me! But they didn't and soon others asked for their pig — then others — and this is how the world-famous PIG-HILL-OF-FAME was born! Just that innocently and simply.

Before long there were 137 pigs on the hill!

## OSCAR POOLE

Two Associated Press reporters stopped by to eat. They enquired about the pigs on the hill. I told them what I just said above. I noticed the lady was making notes as I spoke. "We're from the Associated Press," she said. "And we sense a story here!" That was Thursday, and by Sunday we were in over 1,000 newspapers world-wide — a picture of me in the midst of the pigs!

And, the business DOUBLED in ONE DAY — that day from about $500 to $1,000! "Help, HELP!"

From there it has grown to ten times that amount and still growing!

While several were laughing at our silliness and tackiness, a traveler from the Swedish Embassy in Washington D.C. stopped by. He was *taken* by our place. "This place is so tacky, it's classic!" he said. "This is the most Americana place I've seen throughout my travels."

I asked him if he would write this to the local Chamber of Commerce, which he did, and that has become a prized document and is on permanent display in our restaurant! The man was the "cultural counselor" for the Washington, D.C. Swedish Embassy.

So now we are "cultured" — a new kind, with "folk art" and all! There became a little less laughing. The "so tacky it's classic" has become one of our legendary trademarks. It has stuck!

I saw we had something here. Who wouldn't? This was folk art and I was the artist!

Moby heard about the pigs and sent word that he wanted one. (Moby is the number one country-western disc jockey in America, and at the time, 1992, was associated with Kicks 101.5 in Atlanta.) For the next three months that's all he talked about — his pig on Poole's Hill! So, we made him the "Chief Pig" — a large pig on top of the hill. He remains there today.

## *Pat Buchanan for President*

Then Pat came! In February of 1992 he began his entire southern crusade at our BAR-B-Q with national and international coverage! I was standing with Pat and Shelly at the front door as they walked out, a reporter snapped a picture of me with them holding their pig — it was on the front page of the *San Francisco Chronicle* the next day as well as hundreds of others! Five hundred people gathered in one day at our "tacky" place.

Media from, all over the world — literally — covered the event. CNN, ABC, NBC, CBS, AP, CBC, Reuters, newspapers, magazines — even M-TV (I would not have believed this one unless I had seen it with my own eyes, sitting in our PIG-MOBY-IL).

## Oscar Poole

By now you are asking, "What's going on here? Is all this true? Is it for real?" If you are asking this, what do you think was going on within me?

I am giving you just a little of our story — especially in the early stages — to show you that while Edna and I were continuing with the "menial" work, God was "showing the world what He would do," as He SAID!

One day a reporter stopped by and asked, "How does one get on the hill?" I responded immediately in the *THEN* moment, spontaneously — having never even thought about it before — "You must qualify in three ways: You must have an honest face, good intentions, and $3.00!" (It has since gone to $5.00.)

This is still the answer people receive when they ask the question!

The BAR-B-Q continues today — growing — ever expanding (even as Edna and I are in our motorhome in Beckley, West Virginia! These pages are being written here!)

The restaurant now seats 180 inside with 30 or 40 on the "snoutside!" There is a new paved parking lot surrounding the edifice with the hill moved back to accommodate more pigs! In fact, we took 4,000 little pigs (they are now made of plastic to last longer) and made them into one giant pig shape, perhaps the size of 40 or 50 billboards! This, I think, has become our "signature-pig!" (See our story on www.bbqpilgrim.com/stories.)

Col. Poole's Georgia BAR-B-Q has become a landmark and legend "in the mountains of north Georgia!"

The eatery is known as the TAJ-MA-HOG, the HOG ROCK CAFÉ, and the world-famous PIG-HILL-OF-FAME! Sales have soared into the millions and we are still expanding!

## *The FORMAT changes!*

From "church" to "BAR-B-Q!" Like nearly everyone else, earlier in life I thought that God lived and *did His work* inside church buildings — stained glass, organ sounds, and all the rest. I did not realize that *not only* did God live inside churches (that is, he was enclosed in a box), but He was OUT IN THE WORLD! Where life is! Plain ordinary world! Nature, woods, rocks, trees, oceans, mountains, wind, snow, and rain! He dwelt in business and politics (of all things!), but in my case, He seemed to dwell in a little shack beside the road! A little one at that! Eight feet by twelve feet! He not only lived *in* it, but worked *out* of it! From a roadside shack to a modern day legend!

This surprised me! I had to have *divine direction* to believe it. It came to me progressively and slowly as I responded to that inner voice — and lived out of that voice! I think this may be the greatest accomplishment of my latter years! Listening to God! Inside myself, not from outside sources like books, friends, institutions or even teachers. Amazing! I think what I am saying to you is to live out from yourself! In this area I resonate with Walter Russell, the creative genius of the past generation. Russell died in 1965, but he is as relevant today as he was in the first half of the 20<sup>th</sup> century. To discover Walter Russell, simply "google" his name. I heartily recommend you get acquainted with him! I need to SHOUT this to you!

The point is: Get acquainted with yourself. In so doing, you will become acquainted with God! Because that's where He is! *Within* you! Not OUT THERE, but IN HERE! Within you!! I can't say this LOUDLY enough! This is what Socrates said over 2,000 years ago — "KNOW THYSELF!"

You can see that for me, this whole thing — the BAR-B-Q business with its "iconic" successes — is DEEPLY SPIRITUAL! It's out of the Spirit *speaking inside* me! I know this to be true! And the same is for you! Your success, the achieving of your goals, will come from out of you! Simplistic or no, this is my message to you no matter what your situation may be!

There are untapped resources WITHIN YOU! I want this to be the *central message* of this book! This is my purpose for living ... to turn you on to that *creative genius* locked up inside you! In the words of Walter Russell, you are a genius at "something!" We all are! Dr. J.B. Rhine of Duke University said, "You are a *potential* genius!" You might not know it. If you have not yet discovered yourself, that's the problem! It's there for you! I believe my life is proof of what I'm saying and it is to this end that I am releasing this book! If I can, you can! There is no question about it!

This is what La Vie is about! If we cannot hold the crowds at La Vie we'll come to your city or home!   Go to www.oscarpoole.com and click on "La Vie!" Let's get acquainted! My e-mail address is: oscarpoole@aol.com.

## *"A Rhema Word"*

I want to discuss what some of you know as a "rhema" word. That is, sometimes God speaks through a written word (the "logos word"). Sometimes one may read a verse from the Bible and the spirit within enlivens it — makes it come alive! But even this making it alive is a form of a direct communication.

In this case note a Bible verse in Rev. 12:11. Here's what I heard within myself. "They (that's us) overcame him (that's the adversary — my views about a *devil* and *evil* have changed — but there are adversaries or obstacles to overcome) by the blood of the Lamb (that's the price that God paid for all this) and by the WORD (spoken or released) of our TESTIMONY (truths we have experienced or lived out')." This is not theoretical or oratorical sermons, but practical theology. I call it theology that hits the road! (Our road being Highway 515!) This verse needs *pondering over* many times!

## *Testimony*

As I have indicated earlier, I believe testimonies have taken the place of preaching — simply sharing what God has said and done within and through you! (The Mormons, whom I respect highly, have proven this!)

## Oscar Poole

As Rev. 12:11 was coming alive within me, I heard God's voice directly, "I am building a testimony through you ... when it is finished you can tell others (testify)."

I began to see that this was even how the Bible was written! That they *did* it — then *wrote* about it! They didn't have a theology for writing the Bible! Except a few had scrolls of the Old Testament (very few — the original 12 disciples didn't, I think it is safe to say).

They were led from within themselves — by the Holy Spirit who had come to in-dwell them! Just like it is with you and me.

I referred to this in the earlier book, *"Speak-To-It!"* when I told a *dead* group of orthodox Christians in New York once, "for what we (Travis Tatum and I) were doing, the theology had not been written!" I was embarrassed, but I have discovered that this is true.

Robert Schuller, I had noticed, had proven this. He *lived* it and then wrote about it. This has become an indelibly impressed insight that developed within me as I lived out and moved forward as I was spoken to and led from within myself.

So, to make a longer story shorter, we are now telling and writing about all these matters — a testimony.

Well, it's simple — there was nothing to tell about in 1992 regarding the events that have happened since, but only conjecture! Now, after 20 years, we have something to tell about. We have experienced — lived — everything I am telling you.

I mention again Einstein, regarding the "20 years" mentioned above. God, the *eternal* constant, works through space-time-matter-motion, at least as far as this earth plane is concerned. It takes time — quality time.

This makes God relevant (related) to all that is. Another way of saying it — the spirit works through space, time and matter, and *moves* at varying frequencies!

Repeat: What you actually experience — what you accomplish is your *testimony*! The BAR-B-Q is mine! After you live it, you can tell it! Draw conclusions and observations from it! That's what I am doing now. I have lived it! Now I am telling it! And am I ever! After all, I'm now 79 years young!

## Back to the BAR-B-Q saga

While we were renting the one-third acre lot, we managed to buy the other lot next door, which had a little house on it, for $45,000. We were expanding, Oscar-style! Later, the owner of the one-acre behind us agreed to sell us his parcel. After that we purchased the original lot. Added together, we owned nearly two-acres of high priced land on the four-lane highway, where the world passed by, with the added benefit of a paved parking lot out front, a *park* and *ride*, that the county and state had prepared for commuters to park their cars on Monday through Friday. But what about Saturday and Sunday? You guessed it! Customers from Atlanta for Poole's BAR-B-Q parked there!

Can you see "DIVINE SYNCHRONICITY" at work here on our behalf? A quarter million dollar parking lot, created from dirt out of the mountain where we placed our stand! The Bible calls this "GOD WORKS ALL THINGS TOGETHER!" (Romans 8:28)

How can I tell this whole story of the BAR-B-Q? I can't! I can tell only bits and pieces. It is a Cinderella story — spiritual from the word "Go!" Let's discuss the "spiritual!"

## *Meditation*

I had developed a system of meditation, which I call "confessions of faith" (affirmations). Remember the cat story back in Fayetteville? When I lay on the floor of the tool shed mumbling at 5 a.m., "I am FAR from oppression!" I think that what was born out of adversity has grown into a methodology that anyone can use when facing obstacles and achieving goals. It is the power of words, placed in one's mouth and spoken in meditative fashion!

## *"What concerns you?"*

I was walking one of my three-mile walks one day when I was muttering — meditating and saying out loud repeatedly — "The Lord will perfect that which concerns me" (Psalm 138:8).

Following one of these repetitions, I heard the voice from inside ask, *"What concerns you?"*

That was back in 1993, 16 years ago. I mention the date because God works through space-time-matter and -motion (Einstein). This is illustrated in nature as seed, time and harvest! When you plant a seed (potential) into the ground, it takes time for it to come into fruition or harvest. This is a basic spiritual principle in life itself. Another example would be the research scientist who gets an idea, which he labels a thesis, then proceeds to work it out! Yes, time is involved even in the creative process.

In Genesis the creation story is given in time increments of six days. Not literal 24-hour time frames, but much longer duration, that is, according to my view. Even God had to have time to work things out!

I put together a rather long list of concerns which I began saying back to the personal voice within! Oddly His (God's), First Force (according to Harold Cober), Energy (Einstein) — take your pick! My choice is God! I made this list a part of my daily meditation for the next seven years, and I began to see or realize some of these concerns immediately — as well as a host of them later!

They were practical, everyday things that I really wanted to see happen! I have come to believe that this is spirit-working-out, or manifesting itself, into the world of matter, although I am sure there is a better, scientific way of saying it. A creative process, making itself known into the daily affairs of men! The

God-force gently, sometimes in bursts, rising from *within* (there's that word again).

I am trying to find a simple way to say this! Let us say that it is the Kingdom of God *within* us, working-out or MAN-ifesting God or Spirit into and through the material world.

One gets an idea. He gets it from within. Though the source is not he, it is God — the Divine Force or Spirit. This Divine Force speaks a word or phrase or even a picture or image. We call this in-SPIRIT-ation. I realize that even as I speak this I am writing in mysteries! I am trying to describe the process that seems to be going on within one as an inspirational idea is being birthed.

When gestation (another metaphor) is complete it is ready to be spoken! When it is spoken (released from the spirit) strange and wonderful things begin to take place! The idea begins to MAN-ifest itself. It begins to take shape (or form). It is beginning to formulate!

The mystery *becomes greater* as the process continues! Others hear about it through some mysterious connection. God is working to bring this new thing about! It seems like the powers-that-be begin to converge, working in harmonious patterns to cause this (or these) things to happen! But happen it does and the person with the original idea finds that he did not really cause this new thing to happen although he played a major part! He does have the satisfaction that he was the first to know about it! This gives an inward sense of joy and satisfaction that he helped to birth a creative idea! And the more children he has, the happier he gets! (More metaphors — creative ideas, we'll call the next word in this trilogy, "invention" — notice even that word, "IN [within] -VENT [wind or spirit] -ion." A breath of the Spirit within! It all seems so simple to me!)

Back to my concerns list. I memorized what concerned me. This was not hard to do because they were for real! They were dreams and aspirations (notice the root word spirit again! Everything flows out of the spirit!). I said them *aloud*, repeatedly until they were almost automatic though they never sounded like merely rote words. I could sense a wonderful witness on the inside as I spoke these concerns. This *inside witness* is difficult to explain and I think I know partially why — it is beyond the intellect or mind, it is in the spirit, where sometimes words lose their meaning! I sometimes use the word "feeling" to describe this as contentment, peace, an at-ease-ness, a quietness, a profound satisfaction — but I think that even expressions of emotional feelings are not adequate. Hence I have come to use the word *sense*.

Anyhow, let me say that there is *great joy* on the inside when you sense the spirit working! I find myself very inadequate trying to describe the workings of the Spirit as they are beyond words, or the intellect. I suppose it's impossible — but you know when it is there! You know, like you have experienced something too great to describe! I believe this happens to all of us!

OSCAR POOLE

## *"I want you to write it down!"*

So, I did. I scratched all of these concerns onto a legal-sized paper. Both sides! But that was not enough. I wrote down more concerns, things I wanted to see come about in my life — many times I thought it was too late, since I had finished my professional preaching career. Little did I realize that with God time was of little significance! What I was about to witness was the unfolding of a miracle! Only the *form* was about to change. From a building with a steeple on it — looking up — to one with a pig on it — looking out. Little did I realize that many of the dreams and visions I had carried with me since childhood were about to take place! Not through a church, but through a roadside business. And a tacky one at that!

I named my concern list my "Magna Carta." After much usage the pages were tearing and the edges wearing off so I decided that if they were to last I had better place them in our safety deposit box at the bank. This I did and there they lie for our posterity — this is the value I place upon them!

I say "Magna Carta" because it seemed to me it became a document that laid out sort of a blue print for the remaining years of my life — although I was just getting started in a new career at age 59! I thought of Col. Sanders of fried chicken fame. He was 65 when he hit the road with a sack of flour in the back of his '46 Ford! So, at least I had a six-year jump on him!

I have made some copies of my Magna Carta and I am going to print one here in this book! It does not resemble the rag-tag original in the safety box. Further, it is, at points, a paraphrase of the original, but in *essence* it is a duplicate.

I need to mention about a scripture that *came alive* in all this! This is another example of a rhema word — a scripture made alive — that I mentioned earlier. It is Habbakuk 3:1-3, when the prophet declared, *"Write the vision, make it plain upon tablets, so he who sees it may run with it!"*

Let me explain that the original word that I heard within myself was not a coming alive of this scripture. Rather, it was a direct voice spoken to me in a distinct clear voice — the one I had heard many times before! The scripture here given is merely an affirmation of what I had heard directly! My conclusion? I'm not the only one to whom God had spoken these words!

This has two effects upon me. It prevents me from a "cocky" attitude — that I am above or superior to someone else — but it makes me feel that I am included in very good company! He speaks like this to all — He is no respecter of persons — to you and me. I don't think you have to hear a voice to write down your dreams, concerns and goals. Just *do it!* About every self-improvement psychologist I know of agrees that we should write down our goals.

I don't like the word "secular," as I believe all is spiritual — but for the sake of explanation I will use it here. Modern secular psychology agrees with scriptural declarations, and why not? If you get your historical perspective focused clearly you will know that it was theology that gave birth to science. <u>Truths in science — in this case, psychology — merely affirm</u>

<u>truths in the Bible or elsewhere, as truth begets truth and remains truth no matter where it is and in whatever form it appears!</u>

# *My Magna Carta*

*"The Lord will perfect that which concerns me"* (Psalm 138:8). I added *"and is perfecting,"* as I understand God works through time, matter, space and at a certain speed (Einstein).

*"La Vie in Georgia, an international retreat center."* (La Vie now sits on 12 acres of choice north Georgia mountain land given to me, is incorporated and I am president of it.)

*"Car tags from all over the United States, Canada, Mexico and many foreign countries. A great gathering or coming together.*

*"Hand clap offerings. Anointings.*

*"Orchestras, trumpets, bugles, pianos, organs, flutes, marching bands, tambourines.*

*"A TALL TOWER* (building) *with a chapel and office on top for PERSPECTIVE.*

*"Expectancy. Great numbers. Positive faith. Excitement. Enthusiasm. Youth. Children. Senior citizens* (I now am one!). *Good will.*

*"Vision. 'Writing and running with it!'* (I write the vision, the people — thousands — run with it. They tell it while I sleep!)

*"Books, booklets* (this is one of them), *pamphlets, newsletters, newspapers, cassette tapes, T.V. exposure* (so many times I have lost track!), *radio networks* (all over the world), *magazines."* (Added: *the Internet and E-mail*)

\*Note: When the Pig-Hill-of-Fame was birthed I simply thought of it as a part of this "writing the vision!" Anyhow, the people run with it, and thousands run to it!

*"Entertaining groups. Playing the piano.* (Wherever our motorhome goes, this occurs!)

*"Travel. Much by car, jet, and by bus.* (I guess the R.V. is the bus. It is a class A and looks like one.)

*"Retreats. Seminars. Celebrations. Rallies.*

*"RESPECT. Amongst my peers and the Christian world.*

*"WEALTH, RICHES & HONOR in my household. House bought and paid for.* (It was debt-free the day we moved into it.) *Retirement secure. The knowledge of witty inventions.*

*"Super great favor with God and man.*

*"Superabundance of wealth to establish God's covenant.*

*"Good food for Edna and me, at home and eating in fine restaurants.* (Although I now prefer eating in the hole-in-the wall places!)

*"Mingling and meeting professional people — doctors, attorneys, dentists, educators, governors, presidents and their wives, judges, senators, statesmen, dignitaries, and uncommon common people.*

"*Good clothes for Edna, me, our children, and our seeds' seed perpetually.*

"*Good HEALTH for Edna, me, our children, and our seeds' seed perpetually.*

"*Two-tone blue Cadillac bought and paid far.* (We now own two Cadillacs but neither one of them is blue!)

"*All the fruit of the Spirit. Love, Peace. Joy. Happiness.*

"*Prosperity. Success. Achievement. For God's glory. To tell others so they can be healed, set free, and become "plantings of the Lord."*

"*Hallelujah! Praise the Most High God! Through the SPIRIT!* (Note the praising and thanksgiving twenty years before the manifestation! This illustrates that God, the Eternal Constant, operates or brings into actualization, through time-space-matter-motion — Einsteinian!)

"*Beautiful relationships within the family and in-laws.* (Some of this is in PROCESS! Edna and I have been married 59 years! We courted two years before that!)

"*Romance in our marriage. Enjoyment of each other.*

"*In the NAME of Jesus Christ.* (I have since added "Elohim, Spirit, the I AM ... total DEITY).

"*Thank you Father, for bringing all this ... and more to pass!*"

The above '"Magna Carta" as I said earlier, became sort of a blue print or guide for the years that have followed! Life has

THERE'S ONLY ONE

seemed to be an outflow of these concerns spoken *out loud repeatedly* (see *"Speak-To-It!"* for a more detailed account on meditation).

Not all of these dreams have been accomplished or fulfilled, but most of them have come to pass! Especially is this true in associations with "statesmen, educators, doctors, governors, great numbers, books, booklets, cassette tapes, T.V. exposure, radio networks, magazines, much travel, respect, super great favor, good health for Edna and me, prosperity, success, achievement," ... all this and more!

And it seems like every day the abundance of this increases. Of course, the form of our life's fulfillment has changed from a church building to a BAR-B-Q building. Do you think that I restricted the flow of God's success through us by limiting God in the old churchy form? I wonder! I do not really know, but I can't help but think about it. We did well while in the church syndrome. In fact, I loved much of it ... the preaching, interpersonal relationships, and the changing of lives. But the same has and is happening through this very different form, which has become my forum. I speak to quite large rallies, one-on-one relationships, counseling, write books, play the piano, teach seminars and all the rest of the good stuff without the old boring board meetings, church fusses, negative programs, etc. Now it's all positive atmosphere, almost totally.

There is great joy amongst us, as much of what we do is termed "silly." PIG-MOBY-IL, TAJ-MA-HOG, HOG ROCK CAFE, and the PIG-HILL-OF-FAME! Families gather. People laugh. The atmosphere itself draws people in and many say their lives have changed for the better. The people return and an expanding family-atmosphere dominates! You can sense or feel it!

All because we had the vision, thought it, talked it. Every time the vision or idea is spoken, more happens! You see it's not just the original thinking and speaking — it's the continued speaking by the hundreds and thousands that have become involved. This, I think, has much to do with the exponentiality of our growth! Others working with you.

Keep in mind the Magna Carta was simply the "writing down" in a response to the question of deity (God) into the inner being of one person, me. It has been nothing less that a thrill to see this thing unfold — still in process!

Do you have a Magna Carta for your life?

For a somewhat more detailed explanation of this devotional part of my life, see the second half of my book, *"Speak-To-It!"* on "CONFESSIONS OF FAITH!" This, I think, *could be* one of the *greatest contributions* I have to offer the reader! It is strong! Revolutionary! It will "turn you loose" to discovering yourself and what you CAN DO! I really believe this.

## *Calling things*

You see, I was prophesying the BAR-B-Q legend for years and didn't know it! The POWER of words! (See my book *"Speak-To-It!"*) I was involved in Abrahamic faith. In fact, I had a vision! I don't know why I said those things. It was just "in side" me. The BAR-B-Q was to be in God's scheme-of-things. The basis for this is found in scripture, Romans 4:17: "Abraham CALLED things that WERE NOT as if they were until they BECAME!" This is what I did!

Before I go any further, let Edna (my wife of 59 years) speak. "For years Oscar talked about having a little BAR-B-Q place. When we passed by a BAR-B-Q we found ourselves eating there! Seems like he wanted to stop at all of them! Even after we had our little BAR-B-Q he would still want to try them out! Of course, I was tired of eating BAR-B-Q, but not he!"

When I first saw the little 8' x 12' shack with "BAR-B-Q" on it, I shouted out to Edna — "There it is ... they have MY IDEA!" So we bought it! Went in debt $35,000 and set it up in a couple of places and almost went broke! We were in desperate need for a place to put the mobile rig.

We found it! Right in the middle of East Ellijay!

## *Pat Buchanan*

It was January 1992. Fred Bailey and I were visiting at Joe McCutchen's office and Joe declared he was supporting Pat Buchanan for President. After a thorough discussion Fred and I decided so would we!

A vision emerged as we were talking ... that if we would go to New Hampshire and actively "campaign" for Pat that he would return the favor by coming to Georgia (as it was the state immediately following). We were acquainted with Jack Thrift, Pat's Georgia state chairman, and we had great favor with Jack. Jack had promised Joe McCutchen he would bring Pat up to ELLIJAY to appear on Joe's radio show. (Joe since hosts a weekly television show on ETC-TV.) So, why not drop by Col. Poole's BAR-B-Q?

Fred and I both drove up to New Hampshire to join Pat's supporters. We made phone calls, ran errands, and made many public appearances with one walking around a T.V. appearance dressed in my yellow suit! The folks back in Atlanta were gathered together and watching very closely. "There's Oscar," someone shouted. That did it! While I was still in New Hampshire Jack Thrift put together a scenario for Pat Buchanan to visit our BAR-B-Q!

## *Our "Day of Infamy"*

That's what I call it! Early February came ... and so did Pat! It stretched out over three or four hours and during that time 500 people came and went! The media came — practically all the networks.

I was the host! Pat and Shelly ate BAR-B-Q in our rickety shack. I gave them a pig as they walked out the front door. This was seen on the front page of the *San Francisco Chronicle!*

T.V. networks. Newspapers. Magazines ... important people. A roadside shack and PIG-MOBY-IL "seen around the world!"

Incredible! But true! Here we were, hosting a candidate for President of the United States! A day we cannot forget!

When Pat returned in 1996 and 2000 each rally was covered on national television, C-SPAN as well as other media. Of course, history reveals that Pat lost the election — but Col. Poole's Georgia BAR-B-Q WON! And, won BIG! Front pages ALL OVER THE WORLD! Can the reader believe the words you are reading? (Pretty hard even for us who were there!) I will be eternally grateful to my dear friend, Pat Buchanan and his contribution to this success story!

## *Long Beach, California*

At the Reform Party that nominated Pat Buchanan for President. I went as a delegate (dressed in my yellow suit, of course) and "made the rounds again!" My picture on the front page of the *Los Angeles Times,* CNN, C-SPAN and so many I lost count! I had to wear the yellow suit for several days as I had only one! (Could not afford but one — now I have three!) One day Shelly asked me (aboard a private ship) "how many yellow suits do you have? I remember I was embarrassed to admit that I only had "one"!

Now with presidential candidates, Associated Press, national media, we became something of an institution! These folks who made fun of us did not know that I was a fairly educated man behind these shacks (we added a shack to a shack to a shack)!

## Oscar Poole

We were growing ... and MAKING MONEY! Working hard but having fun doing it!

We kept the "overhead down!" You could reach the ceilings! No monthly payments (except the $35,000 we owed the bank)!

Let me tell you about the first room we added to the original 8' x 12' shack. It was a 10' x 10' added room with the roof from off a chicken house! We placed two cardboard tables in the room for "inside seating!" (Now four could eat inside besides the 35 under the trees.)

Then we added another room which seated 25! It was a room that Fred Bailey gave me on his farm. Of course, I had to dismantle and rebuild it. After that I added a back screened porch seating 25 more! One day I walked in the back door and there sat former governor Lester Maddox who became one of my dearest friends!

I discovered that our "tackiness" drew in the rich folks — sort of like FDR's Little White House down in Warm Springs, Georgia. People love SIMPLICITY and did we ever have that! Of course, the food must be good and the place clean. Well, I am married to Edna and that takes care of that!

## *Where did the name PIG HILL-OF-FAME come from?*

Out of the mouth of Dick Martin, PR man (worldwide) for Lockheed Aircraft!

I was in California attending a retreat. Edna told me over the phone that Dick Martin was complaining: "WHERE'S MY PIG?!" I said, "I'll take care of that as soon as I get home!" I did! I placed it over the front door! Our then manager saw Dick over at Wal-Mart and told him "There's a pig with your name on it at the BAR-B-Q!" Within minutes Dick arrived at the BAR-B-Q!

He saw his pig..."DICK MARTIN"... right out IN FRONT for all the world to see! Dick came alive! Excitedly, he said, "Let's make this place famous! Like out in California where they put footprints in the sidewalks (Hollywood and Vine), or like the VARSITY in Atlanta!"

I chuckled as he spoke.

Dick looked toward the hill, which had a few pigs scattered on it (there are now 7,000-8,000) and said, "Let's call this the PIG HALL ... no, HILL-OF-FAME!" It has been called that ever since. Now you will see about 5,000 little plastic pigs combined into ONE BIG PIG (100' x 50'). This combined pig has become our signature pig. You should see it all lighted up at night — About the size of 40 billboards! Remember when I couldn't get a sign on the highway?!

## *A few words from Edna*

After we opened the BAR-B-Q on June 8, 1989, during October we had our first Apple Festival and didn't know much of what to expect (as the festival was held on the other side of town). Little did we know that the whole world was beginning to come to ELLIJAY!

Guess what? Oscar went out of town for the day to attend some meeting and I was at the BAR-B-Q all by myself! I had to take orders, prepare the food and collect the money! But along came Greg, our son, with his three-year old daughter, Jordan. (He was bringing her up to the Apple Festival.) Seeing my situation, he never made it — he was a God-send! (On a subsequent Apple Festival we fed 1,800 people in one day! Oscar has been present ever since and we hire 20 employees to handle the crowd!)

One day, while working at the carry-out window Dale Wasson appeared. When he approached, I said, "Where have you been all my life?" (I don't know why I said that!) Dale has been our dear friend ever since! He spoils us by cooking cuisine meals for all our workers on frequent occasions — We love you, Dale! He is one of those 20 workers who helps us at all the Apple Festivals!

## *A theology for BAR-B-Q*

I believe a person's BELIEF SYSTEM determines his attitude and actions! His THEOLOGY! (What would you expect from a theologian?!)

In fact, I want to compare WHAT I SAID (over 25 years ago) with what has happened since. If the reader will compare my MAGNA CARTA written in my book, *"Speak-To-It!"* you can clearly see that the actual history is a WORKINGS-OUT of that document.

A cornerstone of my theology is "CBA" — What the mind can CONCEIVE, the heart BELIEVE, you can ACHIEVE! (This is the name of my website: www.wcba.tv.)

I cannot overemphasize the "theology" part of this book! You MUST UNDERGIRD YOUR LIFE WITH YOUR PERSONAL BELIEF SYSTEM! I said these OUT LOUD in what I called CONFESSIONS or AFFIRMATIONS OF FAITH (See my book, *"Speak-To-It!"* for the entire MAGNA CARTA.)

Every successful life must have at its roots a positive belief system. I offer the reader our restaurant experience as "proof" of mine!

## *The John Baeder painting*

Sometime during 1995 I received a phone call from John Baeder, an artist of nostalgia who painted mostly old diners across the country. Someone had sent him a picture postcard of our place. John asked me if he could paint our restaurant. I replied, "Of course!"

Within a few days John arrived at Col. Poole's Georgia BAR-B-Q and took several photos.

It wasn't but a few weeks that John called back and said the 44" x 66" oil painting was "ready!" So, Edna and I traveled to

## Oscar Poole

John's home in Nashville, Tennessee, to witness the "unveiling"!

The next thing I knew the painting was hanging in a New York City art gallery! New York City?! Yes, New York City!

Col. Poole's BAR-B-Q was now seen in a cultural art gallery way up in New York City! You talk about culture! An oil painting by a leading American artist! The value of the "treasured" work-of-art (to us at least) was reported at $40,000! The entire BAR-B-Q was not worth that much!

Somebody told me this was American "folk art"! I think this had quite an influence upon me! Not only was our roadside shack painted by a leading artist, but had it not been for me, there would have been nothing to paint!

The painting now hangs (and is owned by) the MORRIS ART MUSEUM in Augusta, Georgia, with, of course the caption "Col. Poole's Georgia BAR-B-Q, Inc."

So, you see, this "Cinderella Story" moves right along! The day the museum had John Baeder and me in Augusta for the unveiling, the mayor of the city proclaimed me the "MAN OF THE DAY!"

Wow! And WOW! Can you begin to see how incredible this unfolding drama is?!

Often I feel that I'm just going along for the ride! And what a ride it has been ... and, STILL is!

THERE'S ONLY ONE

## *The Washington D.C. story*

(U.S. Congress — 13 consecutive years)

Both Houses of Congress, that is! What an honor to serve our Georgia BAR-B-Q for 13 years in our nation's capitol! Quite a feat for a roadside shack, wouldn't you say?!

The first trip was to the U.S. House of Representatives in the Sam Rayburn Building where we fed 450 people. This event was sponsored by Nathan Deal, our Congressman. This was June of 1997.

We arrived on the House side at 5:30 a.m. Pete Castello, Georgia Ninth District Chairman, was driving the U-Haul truck loaded with Poole's BAR-B-Q. The truck was towing a trailer (loaned to me by Bill Bowman) with our soon-to-be-famous pigmobile (yellow and red). I was driving a car right behind it. The ears of the pigmobile pointed toward the capitol building — they looked like ROCKETS! "WHAT'S THIS?!" the security guards asked! Did we have some explaining to do! You see, this was soon after the Oklahoma City bombing! THE POLICE HEADQUARTERS HAD FAILED TO NOTIFY THE POLICE AT THE ENTRANCE! It fell my lot to explain the situation! After a few strained moments we all had a big laugh and the police became our immediate friends. (Of course, they were invited to the noon BAR-B-Q ... and they accepted! Have we been popular with the capitol police ever since!) We unloaded the pigmobile and parked it near the FRONT STEPS of the capitol! (There are a couple of pictures showing the

## OSCAR POOLE

pigmobile on our Web site, poolesbarbq.com, and on the walls inside the restaurant.)

The next year Sen. Paul Coverdell invited the Colonel to serve his BAR-B-Q to the Senate leadership. Pat Wilson, Governor Perdue's representative in Washington, was very instrumental in this event.

For the next 11 years, the Georgia Rehabilitation Association through Pat Wilson and Cheryl Meadows has invited us.

I suppose the highlight of the entire 13-year experience was when the Roll Call media showed up as we arrived on the Senate front steps for both the eleventh and twelfth years and placed Col. Poole's picture on the FRONT PAGE! Two years in a row! Also the picture of Col. Poole dressed in his yellow suit with the U.S. Senate in the background which appears in the Capitol Hill July 2008 calendar — what a way to sum up 13 years of serving BAR-B-Q to the nation's capitol from a simple roadside shack in Georgia! Of course, as you can see from the cover, we are no longer a roadside shack! (You can view these pictures on the Congressional Record photo page at oscarpoole.com.)

Thirteen years of hard work! But what a privilege! It's part of our history that we here at Col. Poole's Georgia BAR-B-Q are most proud. We have become fixtures on Capitol Hill — especially with the capital police — and many others as well!

## *How do you explain*

Such a phenomenal growth?! Of course, there are many factors involved, such as quality products, commitment to treating the customer as number ONE, the family ambience, the MEDIA — but the spiritual stands out above all the rest. (See my book *"God In The Marketplace"*.) I shall never admit to anything else! It's back to "When God spoke into my spirit WITHIN" — I offer this as the FOUNDATIONAL REASON for ALL our successes here at Col. Poole's Georgia BAR-B-Q, Inc.!

## *We want to keep this family legend going...*

This is why we are keeping it in the family. It's too good an enterprise to let someone else come in and ruin it. We are humbly proud ... and THANKFUL to the God-Spirit within us to consider doing otherwise. Edna and I love the place and the people! We spend a great deal of time "hanging around!" I play the piano upon request, mix and mingle with people who have come to be a part of our extended family.

Now it's our sons' turn to "take over the helm!" Darvin has assumed the leadership with more sons to follow.

My passion is now my spiritual retreat center located nearby in Fannin County (see www.wcba.tv or www.OscarPoole.com) — LA VIE (French for THE LIFE). La Vie sits upon 12 acres of choice mountain land with Oscar's new "cabin in the corner of Glory Land!" If you are a person of good will, tired of confrontational lifestyles, desire to ENJOY others in LOVING RELATIONSHIPS — feel free to check us out!

## Why do I stay involved in politics?

I wonder myself! I guess it's just IN ME! I care about my country, my posterity ... and I do have CONVICTIONS! A part of me shall remain, but I do not have an agenda, nor do I want to pursue a leadership role. (I did serve as chairman of the Gilmer County Republican Party for five years.)

I do see a role as a spokesman for the 27 million small businesses in America. You see, this book attests to the fact that I have been there and done that. Also, I feel that I can speak for small town America! THERE ARE LOTS OF US!

In 2008 I campaigned (showed up in my yellow suit) for Mitt Romney in Iowa and four other states. John McCain participated recently in one of our U.S. Senate BAR-B-Qs. So, there you have it! Somewhat involved!

## A summary of the BAR-B-Q experience

The Col. Poole's Georgia BAR-B-Q, Inc. is a twenty-year history of my life from age 59 to the present, age 79. It has been a "journey-of-faith" and the business has become known around the world as the "Pig Hill of Fame!" Tee shirts and bumper stickers have been seen everywhere! Rome, London and elsewhere, the BAR-B-Q sauce has been shipped overseas to Switzerland and other countries. The eatery has been featured on TV around the world! Reports from China and Indonesia — of course wherever CNN and the other national networks are carried. We became popular with the Embassy of Sweden in our beginnings days. We were so strange we became *folk art* — a painting (44" x 66) which hung in a New York City art gallery until it reached its current home of the Morris Art Museum in Augusta, Georgia. This gave us an "aura of sophistication!" From being laughed at to becoming a legend on Capitol Hill in Washington. Some of the original laughing was ridicule — imagine a grown man driving around in a homemade pig mobile! The secret to our publicity I give is "be yourself! *Don't copy others!* That makes you average! And who wants to be average? Not I! If you will be yourself you'll be *unique!* The world needs individuals — not copycats! After all, no one can be you and you cannot be someone else. Stand out from the crowd! Be all you can become in the form your Creator made you! Be different! (Note: don't forget the 13 years of "Taking the Pork Back to Washington!")

So much so that you will *attract* others to you! This is the law of attraction described in the book *"The Secret"* that Oprah made popular a couple of years ago. I wrote about this law before they did in my book, *"The Physics of Spirit!"* Like attracts like. It is a law of nature — of life itself!

We attracted to ourselves famous people, so famous, we became famous! We attracted the media! They told about it — while we slept! All free!

I am convinced and I think my life has proved it, that when you get in tune with yourself, remain in touch with your source, the universal forces show up to help you achieve your life's dreams and goals! This is basic, and it has to be! This is why I call all that we do "spiritual" — it is life lived out of your spirit — in harmony with the Spirit! So much for preaching!

## *The media*

We attracted the media! Over there on the side of the road, along a busy highway, they passed by, saw it (the law of SIGHT, VISION and IMAGERY), turned around, came back and took pictures of it! It's that simple! Not *simplistic* but simple! What may seem to be simple has deep and profound roots! What appears surfacial gives psychologists much work to do in digging out underlying principles of truth!

## *Here's the media we attracted*

Many of these were "feature" stories. Some showed special events. All adding up to the incredible story below!

1. Ludlow Radio Network
2. WSB-Atlanta
3. Moby, 101.5 Kicks, Atlanta
4. The Atlanta Journal-Constitution
5. The Marietta Journal
6. Dalton Georgia Daily
7. Gainesville Georgia Daily

THERE'S ONLY ONE

8. Scores of other newspapers throughout Georgia and the South
9. Rhubarb Jones
10. Associated Press (over 1,000 newspapers)
11. San Francisco Chronicle (front page)
12. Lexington, Kentucky (front page)
13. Dublin, Ireland (front page)
14. CNN - TV (approximately 6 times, WORLD WIDE)
15. M-TV
16. Reuters News Agency
17. CBC-Canada
18. Japanese News Agency
19. Time
20. Newsweek
21. People Magazine
22. Chattanooga TV-3 (feature)
23. Atlanta TV-5 (feature)
24. Atlanta TV-46 (feature)
25. Atlanta TV-2
26. AtlantaTV-11
27. Chattanooga TV-9 (feature)
28. Chattanooga TV-12 (feature)
29. Atlanta Magazine
30. Chattanooga Free Press (front page, color, Sunday Edition)
31. U.S. News and World Report (feature, color)

32. The Big Click (over 10,000 photo entries)
33. Swedish Embassy – "The most truly American enterprise I've seen."
34. Book on Georgia Travels, by Schimmel
35. Times-Courier, Ellijay, Georgia
36. C-SPAN (3 times)
37. Public Broadcasting Corporation (PBS reports nationwide)
38. German Travel Magazine (available in all German speaking countries)
39. Canada Travel Magazine
40. WDUN Radio, Gainesville, Georgia
41. Oil Painting by John Alan Baeder ("New York City art gallery and Morris Art Museum in Augusta, Georgia)
42. Australian National TV
43. Used for special backdrop for drama, Georgia Institute of Technology
44. Magazine, Georgia On My Mind
45. Los Angeles Times
46. New York Times
47. Washington Times
48. Roll Call, Front Page 2007 and 2008
49. Capitol Hill Calendar July 2008
50. Anchorage, Alaska – Front Page
51. Southern Living (two feature stories)
52. Turner South

53. "Barbeque America" by Rick Brown (PBS) shown across America!
54. GPTV (All 10 stations in Georgia)
55. "BBQ Pilgrim" (A Syracuse University project on the Web)
56. The Al Gainey Show (WDUN)
57. The Martha Zoller Show (WDUN)
58. "The Seven Wonders of Georgia" (Atlanta Journal-Constitution)
59. "The Al Franken Show"
60. National Geographic
61. ETC3-TV

I need to say a word about the Al Franken Show! I was approached by Franken's staff when I was a visitor, invited by the Georgia Republican Party, attending the 2004 National Convention in New York City. I had been warned not to have anything to do with this Al Franken guy — that he was mean-spirited and would embarrass you on TV and the radio. When the phone rang at the Ritz-Carlton Hotel, I tried to say, "No," regarding his associate coming to our BAR-B-Q in Georgia and broadcasting live over Franken's daily three-hour show. I could tell they thought we were some kind of unlettered, non-cultured rednecks and they would come south and make fun of us unsophisticated mountain hillbillies! They brought an innocent CD over to test their sincerity. After hearing it I decided to take the risk!

But in the meantime I began to *think* how I might outsmart Al Franken. I did!

# Oscar Poole

I brought in two professional talk show hosts, Al Gainey, WDUN, Gainesville, and Joe McCutchen, ETC3 Ellijay, to help me! Al Franken was no match for them! Instead of Franken intimidating them, the tables were turned and Al and Joe intimidated Franken.

I also prepared some right-wing chicken for Franken's associate, John Marcus. When we came on "live" at precisely twelve noon, John Marcus told Al Franken, "I'm down here in Georgia with some right-wing chicken in front of me — and it's GOOD!" I had clipped the left wings off a few chickens so we could have right-wing chicken on our menu that day! Told all over the world via national radio! All free!

How is that for out-doing Al Franken and getting some national publicity! By the way, my friends Al Gainey and Joe McCutchen felt pretty good about all this! Out-doing a far left liberal from a "bastion of conservatism" — Georgia-style!

## *More attraction — famous people!*

We not only attracted the media, we attracted many famous people! Below is a "partial list" over the twenty years.

    Governor Sonny Perdue
    Senator Paul Coverdell
    Senator Johnny Isakson
    Senator Saxby Chambliss
    Pat Buchanan

## There's Only One

Miss America, Heather Whitestone

Congressman Nathan Deal, 2009 Candidate for Governor

Congressman Phil Gingrey

Lt. Gov. Casey Cagle

Senator Mack Mattingly

Senator Bill Stephens

Congressman Bob McEwen

Lester Maddox

Guy Millner, Candidate for Governor & Senate

John Knox, Candidate for Governor

Herman Cain, Candidate for U.S. Senate

John Oxendine, Commissioner of Insurance, Candidate for Governor

Bill Goldberg, World Wrestling Champion

Ralph Reed

Senator David Ralston

Grover Norquist, president, Americans for Tax Relief (ATR)

Carolyn Meadows, NRA

Pat Wilson, chargé de'affairs for Governor in Washington

State Senator Chip Rogers

State Representative Tom Graves

State Senator Chip Pearson

## The Law of Association

"One is known by the company he keeps!" Steve Spurrier said, "Hang around at the top!" This is the law of association. I have found that, after a while, they will think of you as "one of them!" I have concluded that my "associations" both at the BAR-B-Q and on Capitol Hill in Washington D.C. have shown this!

## Five years as Chairman, Gilmer GOP

There arose a vacancy in the chairmanship of the Gilmer County GOP and I decided, on the spur of the moment, to attend the local county convention — called "A Few Friends". I told them I would serve if elected. I figured that since I had gained some national notoriety I might as well get involved locally! We arrived at the old courthouse a few minutes before 10 a.m. Word had gotten out that I might want to be chairman. You should have seen the "foot-dragging" to begin the meeting! The meeting began several minutes late, as it appeared that if more showed up, this could keep me from becoming chairman. After all, I was "inexperienced" at such and I "didn't know the ropes" about local Republican politics! (Colloquialism for *not knowing anything!*) After covering a few business items, a friend, Mark Millican, stood up and said, "I nominate Dr. Oscar Poole as chairman of the Gilmer County Republican Party!" There was a second and the motion carried! It was as simple as that! I was chairman of the Gilmer County Republican Party! I began attending district and state conventions and began to make my voice known!"

## The 1996 Convention in San Diego

I attended the state convention in Savannah in May 1996. Somehow, I was chosen to be an alternate at the upcoming convention in San Diego! There was not a total trust in me since I had supported Pat Buchanan! They were afraid we'd pull out and form a third party at the convention — which we did not! Lots of drama going on and I in the middle of it!

The San Diego Convention was uneventful except for one day I sat behind a delegate from Augusta with a strange hat! The media swarmed all over him! I said to myself, "You wait 'til I get home!"

Oscar in the U.S. Senate Kitchen

OSCAR POOLE

## *More on the yellow suit*

While in Clermont, Florida, I stopped at the Presidential Museum and found my top hat. I reasoned that it would stand high enough that at least the TV cameras would see the hat! I bought the suit from a lady that Sam Venable told me about in Dacula, Georgia. The red shirt came from a shop over in Dalton.

I wore my yellow suit for the first time at the state GOP Convention in Macon, Georgia. I sat way up in the stands, but I had to go to the bathroom. Timidly I walked across the floor knowing that all eyes were following me! Honestly I felt I might be thought of as some "off the wall idiot" — until later that night I received so many compliments it began to feel good on me! I decided I could remain humble and proud at the same time!

Now, in Washington, D.C., they wouldn't know who I am except for the yellow suit! I believe the yellow suit has proven the importance of *imagery* and *symbolism!* Of course, there has to be someone inside the suit! That's me! I have added a little additional attraction — one I have not used as of this writing — I have placed incognito, concealed inside the suit, a small speaker driven by a tiny MP3 device programmed with upbeat Philips Sousa marching music, so when I make an appearance there is a marching band accompanying me! I have had lots of fun with my yellow suit even though many have taken the suit seriously, and this I like best because it speaks loud words of patriotism and love for America — which I cherish! Besides, it sets me apart, *draws* attention and I like it!

## *2007*

In April of 2007 Edna and I transferred the reigns of our famous BAR-B-Q restaurant to our son, Darvin, who retired from his high school math and coaching career. This was after 18 years of miracles, under-girded by hard work, political rallies, thirteen years to Capitol Hill in Washington, great media attention, but most of all, God's grace and abundant blessings! It has been "spiritual" all the way through! I have committed myself to always giving praise and credit to my source — the God *both* inside and outside us! During those years I have developed a theology for success, which I hope has come through this book!

## *Surprise!*

The famed BAR-B-Q experience caught me by surprise! It was not a church (certainly not churchy) with a steeple, stained glass windows, and such — but it has been a focus for ministry — of getting to know and love persons from all walks of life! The rich and famous to the not-so-rich and less affluent! It has been a learning experience to say the least.

Twenty years of prosperity! From a "shack beside the road" (Hwy. 515, 75 miles north of Atlanta), it has been nothing less than a thrill!

Now our sons, Darvin and Greg, operate the legendary business while I am entering the "telling phase" of it! Remember that voice I heard INSIDE — "They (that's us) overcame him (the adversary) by the blood of the lamb and by the WORDS OF THEIR TESTIMONY!" You are building a testimony (that's something you do) and after it is accomplished you can tell it!

## *The 2000 Convention in Long Beach*

For presidential candidate Pat Buchanan in the Reform Party! Dressed in my yellow suit I made the front page once again of the *San Francisco Chronicle* as well as CNN! After I was elected as a delegate I offered my resignation as chairman of the Republican Party on C-SPAN TV on the front steps of our BAR-B-Q with Pat Buchanan in attendance. Of course, I endorsed Pat on national TV, realizing my career in politics was over! (It was not, as subsequent events turned out!) My rationale was, and still is, that when one cannot follow his conscience, "to hell with it!" It was a conscience thing and four years later I was sort of forgiven when I was invited to be a guest at the Republican Convention in New York City!

## *The 2004 Republican Convention in New York City*

Edna and I were invited to be the guests of the national convention! The sainted Carolyn Meadows, the Georgia member of the Republican National Committee, arranged this act of kindness and off we went to New York City! Let me tell you about it!

I think this experience was a culmination of *hearing* from God, and a natural but spiritual *consequence* to hearing that voice within.

Sometime during 2003 there developed within me the thought or conviction that I should attend all the Republican conventions of 2004 and that I should build the schedule of my year around them. This arose *within my spirit.*

So, March 2004 came and I attended the Gilmer County Convention and was elected as a delegate to both the 10$^{th}$ District Georgia Convention held in Northwest Georgia in April, and the State Convention held in Columbus in May. This growing conviction become so strong within me that Edna and I had two tailor-made bright yellow suits made for these events, at a cost of several hundred dollars!

## *Disappointed*

I tried to have myself elected from both the district and state convention levels to be a delegate to the national convention August 28 – September 2, 2004. I could not get myself elected as either a delegate or alternate — and further, I sensed there was somebody who did not favor my going to the convention. I have a real gift for sensing when something is wrong, but I wrestled with this idea that maybe it was a little paranoia. Anyhow, I began to sense some rejection. (My support of Pat Buchanan four years earlier was not appreciated!)

Oh, by the way, down in Columbus, I was the only delegate whose picture appeared on the front page of the Columbus paper on Saturday morning, and one of the few seen on local television the night before! Could there be a little jealousy amongst some of us? Yes, that thought ran through my mind. It was easy for me to conclude this!

I began to have some doubts about going to New York City. But a real saint entered my life once again — I speak of Carolyn Meadows, our Republican National Committee woman. She said to me, "I want you and Edna to go as my guests!"

I pondered all the terrorist threats being made about disputing the upcoming national process, and I wasn't a delegate. So I wrestled further with the idea of whether to go.

The invitation forms arrived, Edna and I filled them out and gave the state headquarters our visa number and waited. Two months passed and we heard nothing. This added to my concern of spending all that money and then going up there and not being a "part" of the convention!

I prayed. I asked God out loud — "Do you want me to go?" No answer. Then I said, "If you don't want me to go please stop it, put a block in my path so I'll know!" I am revealing this personal struggle about hearing from God to let you know that it's not always easy to hear God speak! Since no stumbling block occurred, we packed our bags and left for New York

City based upon the lack of hindrance plus the earlier conviction of 2003.

## *The Atlanta Airport*

We arrived at the Atlanta airport. I was feeling somewhat freer in my spirit and beginning to feel the excitement that was on the way. I met DeVida, an official with Air Tran Airways who was about the leave for the day and had in her hand a book about God. To make a longer story shorter I told her that I had just written a book, *"Speak-To-It!"* and autographed her a copy. *Connection!* We immediately connected in our spirits! She told me the flights were overbooked, and this led to our giving up our seats and departing three hours later. The airline gave us two round trip passes to as far away as Los Angeles. It *just happened* that Edna and I wanted to go back to see our friends in San Diego — only this time mostly free!

So, I thought to myself, now I have two affirmations that this is a "right" trip. I felt a little freer! You see, the answer to my question about going is coming in stages — not simple and clear as at other times.

## *Arrival*

New York City?! We arrived there in good shape and within two hours were all set up in the fabulous Ritz-Carlton hotel in the southern financial district of Manhattan. Our fifth floor room overlooked the Statue of Liberty!

For the next five days we *wined* and *dined* with top officials of Georgia — the governor, senators, congressmen, their wives (specifically Nancy Coverdell and Leslie Mattingly), party officials and many others.

## *Orientation*

An orientation meeting was held for all delegates, alternates and guests (that's us — Oscar and Edna). Somehow there emerged a feeling of acceptance — that we're all Georgians, here to represent Georgia together. Let me give credit to Alec Poitevant, our state GOP president. He made us all, guests included, feel like family. I have to say, "Thank you, Alec!"

All during this time we are meeting new friends. People we'd never known all of a sudden becoming *connected* and life-long friends. *Expansion!*

We all, over 300 of us, went to see a Broadway play, "Beauty and the Beast!" What a thrill. One happy family from Georgia experiencing this moving play of how love changed a beast into a prince! So, the whole RNC starts out on a spiritual note!

Let me say parenthetically that while Edna and I were promised one pass to one session, we actually received all five passes to all five sessions! See my affirmation of faith in my earlier book, *"Speak-To-It!"* on "I have super great favor with both God and man!" This said twenty years earlier!

## *Why did we go to the RNC?*

Every event needs a purpose — a reason or reasons. First, the one-year-earlier conviction that I should attend the '04 national convention. That's enough reason! That, I take to be of God!

But I have others. I asked myself why I should go, and here's what I came up with:

Number one, I wanted to represent my state of Georgia — to be a sort of a goodwill ambassador. Like my mayor, Mack West says, I represent our little town of East Ellijay!

Number two, I wanted to make more friends and love on more people! I am a people-person and I have within me a profound love for others.

Number three, I wanted to speak to the issues! This I did on network television (U.S., Europe, Far East and Mid-East)! Think about it! A small businessman, an entrepreneur representing all the other entrepreneurs from small town, U.S.A. speaking to world issues!

## *A statement of JOY!*

Number four, Edna and I wanted to make a statement of joy by wearing our bright yellow suits! To let folks know that involvement in politics could and should be an *enjoyable* experience — that one can laugh and have fun while at the same time dealing with survival issues. I believe that each of us gives off *emanations, vibrations, auras,* that we have a *presence* and this presence either *attracts* or *detracts*. We found that it's probably 100 to one on the attraction. Even "liberals" liked us!

Number five, we certainly desired to make media coverage and this we did — probably 200 medias! I will try to list the ones that I know *first-hand*.

## *Media list (2004, New York City event)*

1. First and foremost was the live CNN moment when I was the first person to greet former president George Bush and Barbara Bush as they entered the floor! Wow! Thrill! An eternal moment, with a brief chat. Live national TV!

2. The AP (Associated Press). I am listing these in priority fashion in terms of my thinking. Their photo of me with David Barbee, a delegate from Augusta, Georgia, was covered by hundreds of newspapers throughout the U.S. and Canada — I don't know where else. Harold Shock sent me one from Thunder Bay, Canada (Gerald Scott) and another from Anchorage, Alaska. Front full page — in color!

3. Fox 5 in Atlanta. They covered me playing the piano at the Ritz-Carlton, plus addressing my admiration for Zell Miller!

4. WSB-TV, Channel 2, Atlanta, carried me on the evening news endorsing Zell Miller.

5. TV-46 (CBS) in Atlanta.

6. ABC Evening News with Peter Jennings, report from Glen & Peggy Morton.

7. David Letterman Show, CBS, etc. They were sort-of making fun! But who cares?! Didn't I mention that we were there to have fun?!

8. 60 Minutes, CBS. Third Day, a contemporary Christian music group from Marietta, Georgia, and frequent guests at our BAR-B-Q restaurant, was filmed at our Georgia delegation site, and I happened to be the only one sitting there. The rest were all at a meeting and I, being only a guest, was seated there and the producer asked me if it were okay to use the Georgia sign as a backdrop and I said "Yes!" They allowed me to be a part of the backdrop!

9. MSNBC-TV, report from Pete and Ruth Anna Perry.

10. The Internet — who knows at the millions of people who saw us there?

11. The New York Times wire service showing a great shot of Edna and me with the whole Madison Square Garden with all its festive regalia in the background. This was

the front page full-color of the Anchorage newspaper and hundreds of others!

12. Several New York City television stations.

13. The New York Post— full pictures of Edna and me. A couple at the LaGuardia Airport said, "You're in today's paper!"

14. Other media known by me firsthand: Minneapolis TV, with Senator Tom Coleman, Alabama TV with Senator Shelby, Augusta Chronicle, Atlanta Journal-Constitution, Fox-Houston (a note from Dorothy Halstead), the hundreds of individual photos, perhaps a thousand — returning to their hometowns across America and I'm sure many of them finding themselves in local small town newspapers.

All of the above are media that I know firsthand!

Other media that I remember talking to and being covered by, although I have no idea what they did with it, include UPI, BBC-London, PBSA, Berlin TV, two newspapers in Amsterdam, Swiss TV, Madrid TV, Jerusalem TV, Taiwan TV, New York Times, C-Span, Time Magazine, Newsweek Magazine, Washington D.C. radio, and Al Jazeera TV (that was a "scary" one and you had better believe that after their interview I carefully tried to remember what I had said and hoped I had used good diplomacy). Anyhow, imagine the very possibility of the people in Iraq, Iran, Syria and Saudi Arabia listening to and watching a man in a yellow suit with an American patriotic hat!

Number six: Lastly, regarding why did we go? I suppose it might be to increase our BAR-B-Q business back home in Georgia! I'm sure that's in there somewhere, but you see where I placed it — last. I appreciate our business and of course want to grow, but we have all we need. But growth and expansion are, after all, a part of my theology! But in my heart the other five reasons are far more important.

## *The bus trip*

I must include this! It was the second day of the convention. All the Georgia delegation had gone across town to a meeting. Edna and I in our yellow suits, got ourselves ready by 3:30 p.m. (I mention the time because it was important to what I am about to reveal.)

The buses started to run at 4 p.m., but somehow they loaded Edna and me onto a bus and took off — headed to Madison Square Garden. A delegate had loaned me his floor pass, which was good until 8 p.m. We arrived at MSG at 4 p.m. and we were able to spend the next four hours on the floor of the convention! Keep in mind this amount of time is almost unheard of and after all, we were only "guests!"

During these four hours I experienced a media blitz! I say "I" because Edna got tired and went back to our seats to rest while I "made the rounds." I tried to count the media in my mind and I lost track after about 25 or 30! I believe I am safe in saying that it was 50 or more! And this only during one session!

It was during this floor experience that I was greeted by Mayor Bloomberg, who personally welcomed me to New York City! Pretty "high cotton," wouldn't you say?

But the highlight I am trying to describe here is the bus trip itself! Here were Edna and I, the only two on the bus, with the driver and a police escort. This was a moment I'll never forget! Edna and I escorted on a half-million dollar bus, our own private driver and our own NYPD escort! How could I believe this! We drove through and around police barricades, past a few protesters — right to Madison Square Garden!

About half way to the convention center the thought came to me, "I'll move heaven and earth for someone who is flowing with me — past terrorists, protestors, blocked streets..." This in New York City! I will never forget the moments on this bus trip! Never!

I think I ought to include that in my Magna Carta, I "spoke" of much travel by car, jet and by bus! I'm telling you— there's something to this speaking-to-it!

## *Some concluding observations*

There are so many so I will make them in list fashion.

# There's Only One

1. Edna and I experienced an *awesomeness* to the whole experience.
2. We felt a part of a *right-now* event!
3. The entire process was a challenge for us. From some early apprehension to relief when it was over! I am referring mainly to security.
4. The events — as they unfolded, proved that my one-year-earlier feeling that we should attend was correct — that I had "heard from God" in my spirit!
5. I witnessed the power of *imagery* time after time, right before my eyes!
6. *Spiritual attraction* was at work! I am convinced it was not just the yellow suits — but we had something to say — and the media listened!
7. I learned there is still a place for the "little guy" in the Republican Party. It has helped me to distinguish between a populist (that's me, a person of the people) — and the fat-cat elitist, and we have *both* amongst us! So, I am admitting there is some division in our Republican ranks and this needs to change!
8. I have come to understand my own political stance much better! I certainly am not a "left-wing-socialist-radical" — nor am I a "far-right-ultra-conservative" with no *common sense* values. I see myself as somewhat a "centrist," with neither extreme. I'm not sure I like the term "moderate" but that *might* describe me! Too big a subject to discuss at length here!

Let me conclude by referring back to my Magna Carta one last time, when I heard God say within my spirit, "If you'll get on the side of that hill and do the menial work, I'll show the world what I will do!"

Well, that's been twenty years ago and I think that attending the RNC in NYC August 28 through September 2, 2004, represents quite a culmination of what God said to me many years *before!*

## *2009*

The year is 2009 and on April 29 I turned 79 years of age! At a time when most men my age would be quitting, I seem to only be starting! Life is all too short. I seem to be asking, "Where has all the time gone?" In one more year I will be an octogenarian! This reminds me of the year I was turning 40 — that seemed old to me. Now, how about *double* that? And how much time do I have left?

No one knows the answer to that question, but I have requested 45 more years — I want to be the oldest person on "Larry King Dead!" Let me explain:

On my 70th birthday the BAR-B-Q staff threw a party for me with a big sign out front, "Oscar's 70th Birthday!" While we were seated at a table, a customer said his grandmother lived to be 100! He shared that all the years leading up to the century mark she repeated words like, "If one does not live to be a hundred he is not what he ought to be," as if he or she robs himself of many years! I caught on to her "saying" the words! I had just written my first book, *"Speak-To-It!"* in which I explored the power of words! The power of life and death are in the tongue! I had reprogrammed my vocabulary to speak "LIFE" and not "DEATH." So I thought to myself, "If speaking or saying it, as in the case of the man's grandmother, has anything to do with it, I'll say 117 — no, I'll add seven and make 124 — I want to become the oldest man on earth!"

I know all this sounds silly to many reading this, but silly or not, I have put my request in! It goes without saying that I desire good health, mental alertness and living excitedly, but I'll say that, too! In fact, I have others saying it! They are saying they want to attend my funeral. Edna says she'll have to live until 122, as she needs to be around to look after me! Oh well, time will tell and we'll have to wait around to see!

Oscar making sure the food is fit for a king

Congressman Jack Kingston and Oscar

Pig-Mobile at the Capitol

THERE'S ONLY ONE

Edna, Oscar, Senator Saxby Chambliss

*To Oscar + Edna —
You are great Americans + great friends!
Saxby Chambliss
U.S.S.*

# Chapter XVII
# A New Career

Me? Wait around?

Never!

I have begun my third career — preaching, business and now — I hardly know what to call it! Let's say — Pontificating!

## *The McCutchen-Poole Small Business Coalition*

The truth is, my friend and colleague, Joe McCutchen, and I have formed the McCutchen-Poole Small Business Coalition! This emphasis in my life has been a natural outgrowth from my professional years as a theologian, and the eighteen years as a small businessman. The eighteen years (Darvin has been at the helm for the last two years) grew into my new career!

It seems this direction was led by friendly forces beyond me! It has *come to me* — a phrase from quantum physics! Attraction! We simply grew into it!

It's that *telling* phase I referred to earlier! That voice I heard twenty years ago when I was told to be quiet and listen!

This I did! I was not heard from for several years up here in the mountains! Into the woods I went and stayed, but finally *came out!* These last few words are spoken metaphorically, as much of my woods experience was out in public — at the emerging world-class BAR-B-Q restaurant. I suppose there needed to be a "host of witnesses" to the successful image our lives were taking! Edna and I lived out our success principles on the side of the road for the world to see! The BAR-B-Q became a north Georgia legend and landmark and we (Edna and I, plus others) had the privilege to give direction to it.

## *Legacy*

The BAR-B-Q stands as a symbol of my legacy — what I (remember, it's always "we") have left behind. I'd hate to live this many years and be forgotten! I enjoy being left alone, but not that much! This is the main reason for writing this book — I want to leave a record behind — a trail for others to enjoy and emulate.

I believe the principles that have guided us are TRUTH PRINCIPLES — THEY CHANGE NOT! That's what truth is! They are *constants*. They are generic in nature! What we can do, you can do! We can all be successful — that is, achieve our goals! Especially has this been true here in America. That's the whole idea — to get the government *out of the way* so every citizen of this great land can achieve his *potential!*

Every time I hear the Star Spangled Banner, chills run up and down my spine! I find myself at attention when marching bands come down the street! The same is true with "O

Beautiful For Spacious Skies," "America," and the other great patriotic masterpieces!

"Thine alabaster cities gleam, undimmed by human tears — 'til all success be nobleness!" Who wants to change our system of government for another? The one that has proven to be the greatest peace and prosperity nation in the world? What other?

Of course, we are not perfect. Who said we were? We have many acts to clean up! We need to amend many of our ways, but why destroy the good and the brotherhood of our comrades to obliterate the land that has *attracted* the good, true and the beautiful from beyond our shores? Let's keep what we have, make it better, until every person enjoys the fruits of his labors! Until our grandchildren play around our tables. The auras of peace, brotherhood and prosperity cover us as the "waters cover the seas!"

## *Our way of life is threatened*

These United States of ours — land that we love — is threatened by forces and ideas to make us into some kind of socialist state — the loss of our freedoms and those principles which have made us who we are! It's happening 24/7 and while we sleep these forces lurk *in the dark!*

Legislation passed without being read! As per the recent stimulus package! Whoever heard of that? Imagine our elected officials voting on legislation without even knowing what they are voting on! This is how hidden amendments are slipped in — at night and not ever known it was there until *after the fact!* Such was the case in the AIG "bonuses" at the time of this writing! You can see that something is stirring inside me as I write!

## *Free enterprise vs. socialism*

For decades, especially since World War II, America has been headed in a socialist direction with more control of our lives from the federal government on down to the local level. Too much government at all levels! Rules and regulations galore! Rules to make other rules! Made by University students with nothing else to do but make rules about something they know almost nothing about! Inspectors, after having found fault, publishing their findings in the local media for all the world to see! Even when there might be a legitimate issue it seems to me, it needs to be resolved without hanging out your dirty laundry to wash! *Transparency?* Tell this to the federal government and their passing legislation in the middle of the night!

Big brother increasingly meddling in our affairs! It is no wonder that Grover Norquist wrote a book, "Leave Us Alone," in which he demonstrates "there is no telling how much we can accomplish as free persons when the government leaves us alone!"

OSCAR POOLE

## *Free market control vs. government control*

History has proven that when free market economy reigns *everybody wins!* Hard work, thrift, creative ideas, coupled with a free environment will win every time! There are creative ideas for the solutions of our problems. Just waiting to be received by freedom loving persons eager to "set captives free!" The sky is unlimited!

Vladimir Putin gave warning to the West recently at a summit meeting in Europe, for the government "not to manage the economy!" Imagine: A dire warning from a communist for free enterprise champions to "stay out of business!" In a recent *Pravda* editorial, the Russians *scolded* America for "turning back the clock" to the system that destroyed them!

What will happen when the government goes broke?

We're finding out! "We're already bankrupt," declared Dick Morris less than 24 hours before this writing on a national talk show. We are in uncharted waters — what I saw upon leaving Grand Cayman Island on the rear of a cruise ship just a few years ago!

We are at a crisis!

No one will dispute this. It's like a jungle — full of briars — anyway you turn you get stuck with another! The forces we have set in motion as a free nation have come back to haunt us!

How did we get here? From my perspective I offer five basic causes:

- **NAFTA and GAT trade treaties. We shipped our jobs overseas, leaving our workers with no jobs, now we raise taxes on persons with no income! No revenue for the government to tax!**

- **Corporate Greed! Conglomerates (big business) has become the order of the day! Run the little guy (Mom & Pop businesses) out! The ones to pay the bills (taxes) and employ 70/80 percent of the workers** — while our jobless force increases and crowds grow exponentially at unemployment lines to get their share of "borrowed money!" (Chinese, et. al.)

- **THE CROOKS ON WALL STREET.** I think this reason for the collapse of our economy is obvious. This along with the "Enrons" far from Wall Street.

- **The government itself (Reagan said this!) Agencies that put pressure on the Fannie Maes and the Acorns to lend money to customers who could not afford to repay the loans.**

- **Every person who borrowed money knowing he could never pay back the interest and certainly not the loan itself.**

(See my "talking points" on www.oscarpoole.com for further information on our Small Business Coalition.)

## *More on the McCutchen-Poole Small Business Coalition*

My dear friend and close associate of these past twenty years and I have organized what we call the "McCutchen-Poole Small Business Coalition" — our purpose to excite an *exponential number* of persons to help the twenty-seven million small business owners to become a significant voice in American politics — a force of at least 81 million voters (25 million times 3 equals 81 million!) This is a force and voice that has not been heard from and we believe can help change the direction of our nation! (See Addendum IV)

We are addressing the question: How do we get out of the mess we're in?

I believe that the principles we have emulated in our story of Col. Poole's Georgia BAR-B-Q, Inc. are a solid foundation for any small business to follow!

Gilmer County is the Small Business Capital of the World! Many of us *are making* it so!

# There's Only One

And, why not?

Mr. McCutchen and I are putting together a coalition of local government, educational, media, and civic leaders to create a model of successful ideas-in-action on a small scale (Gilmer County, Georgia has a population of 30,000 plus). We believe we can demonstrate what sound economic policies, family values, and morality-in-government can accomplish when working together! (See oscarpoole.com)

To this end we have been endorsed by all the above: The Gilmer County High School, The Gilmer County Chamber of Commerce, all three of our elected officials, our small town media, the Times-Courier newspaper, ETC-3 TV and WLJA radio! We have formed a consortium to act as a *think tank* for creative ideas to accomplish our common task!

We want to create a *consciousness* that small business can help save America!

An impossible task? If we can be successful here and you over there, and others beyond, we can do it!

You see, there are more of us than there are of them! We are the majority! Let's do it!

OSCAR POOLE

## *Speaking of a Voice in America*

Herein lies the secret! Let's TALK IT UP! All of us together! Everywhere! Out from this will emerge CREATIVE IDEAS to get the job done!

## *Talk Radio*

Here is our tool — talk radio! It is the *little man's vehicle!* So strong and powerful, there are forces lurking that want to shut it up! I speak of the fairness doctrine, which, if implemented, would destroy free speech in America! Words have power and when spoken, activate other dynamics of creativity! When the government controls the media, we've had it! This is our first amendment right — let's not *lose* it, but *use* it!

## *Gilmer County a Model*

The idea of Gilmer County being a model for small business in America came from Paige Green, the leader of our local chamber. You can readily see that our task is bigger than we and we need the help of all who will enlist with us! You can create a group in your area. This movement can become bigger than all of us! That's what we want! When the names McCutchen and Poole become "lost" in such a successful endeavor we will have won!

THERE'S ONLY ONE

You are invited to visit www.oscarpoole.com and to respond as you may wish! Those of us in Gilmer County, Georgia, remain willing to help! Joe McCutchen and I would love to address your group most anywhere!

E-mail oscarpoole@aol.com or mccutchen@mac.com.

Oscar Poole and Joe McCutchen

OSCAR POOLE

# Chapter XVIII
# Summary

To those of you who have read my book I express my heartfelt appreciation! But to those who have helped me live it, I owe you a debt of gratitude I can never repay! To Edna, fifty-nine years living with me — she says she has to live to be 122 as I could never make it without her! (You know my plans are for 124! By the way, do you want to join me?) To our four sons, Keith, Darvin, Greg and Michael — their wives Melanie and Cynthia, to our eight grandchildren: Crystal, Brittany, Jordan, Caleb, Sarah, Stephanie, David and Coleman — I could never have lived my life without you, nor would I want to!

Thank you to all my friends, *both* of them!

Seventy-nine years! That's 34 percent of our nation's history!

Early in this story I reached back to George Washington when my grandfather (three times over) was a soldier under his command. I recently spent a couple of days at Valley Forge where I am sure he camped.

I described how my dad saved his nickels and dimes from the fish he caught while his hand-picked cotton lay in waiting for the sound of the cotton mill whistle to blow.

It was the early influence of *hard work* and *frugality* — along with those Yankees living on my dad's old-fashioned tourist camp — coupled with those God-is-love, spiritual emphases that grew out of the people I loved and knew!

Do I feel old? After nine o'clock at night, yes! But at five in the morning, no! I feel "young and fresh! Ready to start all over again!

Successful minister. Businessman of some repute. Led by sound conservative principles from my childhood.

And now! Telling it! Relating to others how they, too, can become successful and achieve their goals!

This is fun! And exhilarating!

My life has been like a garden! Seed-time and harvest! *Saving, conserving* then spending — *conservatively*, I might add! Frugality has its own benefits! Security, peace-of-mind, enjoyment!

There is enough for all! There is abundance all around us — waiting to be received! For the knowing, asking and receiving!

Remember the quote from Senator Robert Byrd 59 years ago in 1950 in my history class at Morris Harvey College? Man is at a decisive moment (crisis) — he will plunge to his lowest abyss or he will ascend to heights unknown and beyond!

It is this latter that I believe in and am committed to! I have a "theology of hope" a dream of prosperity for all! I am an eternal optimist!

## *Personal Legacy*

- **Five earned degrees**
- **Seven books**
- **Six piano CDs**
- **Built three churches**
- **Organized four new churches**
- **Minister of the year three times**
- **"One of one hundred most innovative and creative" in the United Methodist Church (Nashville, Tydings, 1971). I did not say it, they did!**
- **Legendary BAR-B-Q business, 20 years**
- **Spokesman for responsible conservative principles**
- **Internet radio?**

Special Notice: The following addendums are not guaranteed! When I state that, "man is a sleeping giant waiting to be awakened" (Addendum I, Number 56), I really believe and am committed to this. Standing between *where we are* and *where we can go* lies our free choice — both individually and collectively, the choice is ours! Yours and mine!

THERE'S ONLY ONE

Oscar Poole's Yellow Brick Road to Personal and Business Success

# Addendum I
# New Insights Gained from Listening

The following is a partial list of *new insights* or *revealed* truths received during the years following 1988. Notice that I never leave the *spiritual principles* underlying ALL OF LIFE. I do not distinguish between "sacred" and "secular!"

1. **Basic matter seems to have the capacity to respond to a loving person.**

2. **If it's new, it's now and if it's now, it's new — never having been done before! There are NO PAST MODELS. We are into *uncharted* waters!**

3. **Matter (nature) is "spirit slowed down to visibility."**

4. **We, as spirit-beings, are *connected* into both nature and spirit.**

5. **The created order is in pain, waiting for us to manifest healing and wholeness. Even Scripture attests to this! (Romans 8)**

6. **We can see and do as God sees and does!**

7. We are surrounded by creativity that can be tapped into for the asking. We are submerged into this creativity.

8. We can call things that "ARE NOT" AS IF they were, until they BECOME! We are co-creators with God!

9. Infinite wisdom is available to us! You can see that I am "not about" to leave the "spiritual!"

10. Common or average persons can become uncommon or above average when inspired or enlivened by the Spirit!

11. A special relationship exists between us and all that surrounds us — persons and nature!

12. Love — God's kind (agape-nature) fills our natures.

13. As God is — so are we!

14. Now!

15. Eternity is now (tomorrow will be another now). Live in it!

16. Truth is revealed *progressively*, dependent only upon our ability to receive it.

17. It is spirit-over-mind-over-matter.

18. Genes (as in DNA) can be affected, given direction, or changed. This is a modern *scientific breakthrough*!

19. This is a New Day, Era, or Age.

20. Loving optimism changes pessimism or negativism.

21. Right will win over wrong or evil.

22. Science is a friend to theology.

23. The world of Spirit is vast and unexplored.

24. Imagination (ability to see) determines what we can do!

25. Our self-image determines the extent of our goals.

26. What the mind can *Conceive*, and the heart *Believe*, we can *Achieve!* (CBA)

27. I'm not what I think I am, I'm not what you think I am, but I am what I think you think I am!

28. Love is the commitment to helping discover the *potential* in others. (Frankl and Jesus!)

29. God (Spirit, Deity, Energy) is the ultimate constant but works progressively through space-time-matter-motion. (Einstein)

30. Peace and good will shall cover the earth!

31. We can heal and restore the created code by speaking-to-it!

32. Theology, philosophy and nuclear physiology are connected together in a harmonious relationship!

33. Matter can be filled with spirit — sick and rebellious cells can respond to calls of loving correction!

34. Physical immune systems can be strengthened or enhanced by our words, actions and by medicine (holistic).

35. Our immune systems are strengthened when we *affirm* or strengthen others!

36. We can find ourselves again!

37. Evil cannot triumph over God!

38. Essence is more important than form!

39. Growth, expandability, is the nature of the world of spirit.

40. Exponentiality is God's way of expanding.

41. The secret of the uni-verse is a person.

42. Reality is comprised of loving relationships!

43. Legalism destroys the spirit! It negates truth and stifles creativity!

44. Complaining and criticizing weakens immune systems, slows down creativity and destroys loving relationships.

45. There is a correct time to reveal secrets. A new revelation should be held in secret until the time comes to reveal it!

46. Getting up early is an important factor in success.

47. Success is achieving your goals.

48. A wise person is open for correction.

49. Visions and goals should be written!

50. Living creatively is enjoyable! It makes even hard work fun.

51. Listening is a fine art and must be planned and learned.

52. Truth, the ultimate constant, does not change — but our understandings do.

53. Open minds open the spirit! The choice is ours!

54. Humility, patience and loving-kindness are absolute necessities for progressive journeys of faith.

55. Becoming a genius is not necessarily determined by heredity or environment. It can sometimes be discovered! (Rhine)

56. Man is a sleeping giant to be awakened.

# Addendum II
# Secrets of Success

The following material is what I call my "Secrets of Success." They are taken from a video tape, "Col. Poole's Secret Recipe for Success," a professional television interview with talk-show host Joe McCutchen.

These are statements of philosophy and practical suggestions for achieving one's goals.

1. Tap into your **DIVINE CONNECTION**.

2. **CONTAGION!** Allow these divine auras to emanate.

3. **VISION.** It is progressive and you must have it! You must "see" yourself as successful!

4. **IMAGERY.** What you can **SEE** and **BELIEVE**, you can **ACHIEVE**.

5. **SELF-TALK.** This releases creative energy and gives direction.

6. Do enough **RIGHT** things and **BREAKS** will come your way.

7. **BE UNIQUE.** In our case it was the **PIG-MOBY-IL**, the **PIG-HILL-OF-FAME**, et. al.

8. It's easier to receive forgiveness than permission!

9. **WORK, WORK, WORK!**

10. Maintain a **LOW OVERHEAD**.

11. Be **FRIENDLY!** Smile.

12. The customer comes **FIRST**.

13. Make free use of the **MEDIA**. Ours began with "call-in" radio talk shows.

14. Never be ashamed of your **POLITICAL STANCE**.

15. Stay **FOCUSED** on your goals.

16. Re-adjust goals.

17. **WRITE** your goals.

18. Repeat **POSITIVE** personal declarations of faith. Daily.

19. Food **QUALITY** consistently excellent.

20. Dare to believe even though in a business recession (we began during one in 1989).

21. Willingness to be laughed at! We were!

22. INVOLVE customers' ideas.

23. Have something like a PIG-MOBY-IL.

24. Keep it SIMPLE.

25. We were "so tacky, it's classic!" (Swedish Embassy)

26. Develop a TEAM SPIRIT.

27. Have FUN!

28. Believe and practice EXPONENTIALITY!

29. "Hang around at the top." (Steve Spurrier)

30. Be CONSISTENT.

31. LOCATION, LOCATION, LOCATION!

32. VISIBILITY.

33. ACCESSIBILITY.

34. Receive **CORRECTION**.

35. Maintain a healthy exercise program.

36. **PRAISE** and **AFFIRM** others. (You can stay *healthy* doing this!)

37. Keep the **POWER OF THE SECRET!**

38. Adequate parking.

39. Have three or four trusted **COUNSELORS**.

40. **ASK** for help.

41. Have at least one **JOE McCUTCHEN** as your friend.

42. **CREATIVITY EXPANDS, GROWS, AS** you move toward your goals.

43. Have a **DAPDAE** system:
       D - Data
       A - Analyze the data
       P - Plan
       D - Delegate
       A - Action
       E - Evaluate

44. Every time you set a new goal you create a situation for some creative **TENSION** and **CONFLICT.**

45. **GIVE THANKS — OFTEN!** In fact, overdo it!

46. **SPEAK-TO-IT!** Matter and situations.

47. Sacrifice pleasure for capital outlay; e.g., money spent on cars, invest in property.

48. One success leads to another. You can develop a "habit of success!" (Schuller)

49. Learn to "point!" (Delegate — inspiration from Glen Bowen's father.)

50. Take a trip and "think" about it! (Detachment)

51. Allow your healthy **PERSONA** to develop (a loving presence).

52. Daring to do the **IMPOSSIBLE** is an **ACT OF FAITH!**

53. See **PROCESS** as a goal. Make the journey a success itself.

54. Allow **NEW IDEAS** to come your way and be open to the "good" ones.

55. Again, LISTEN to that voice within and to others.

56. Live in the NOW!

57. Learn how to BREATHE! Inhaling and exhaling can be a refreshing experience.

58. DO NOT SUCCUMB to an elitist attitude.

59. Stay HUMBLE!

60. Don't forget where you came from!

61. Or, the ones who helped you get where you are!

62. DANCE to the rhythms you hear INSIDE!

63. REST daily. Take breaks, naps.

64. **REJOICE AND BE GLAD!**

65. Then WRITE about it! Who knows, you might become a writer!

66. Make sure you keep a diary! Scratch down rough notes. This becomes the basis for your book!

OSCAR POOLE

# Addendum III
# My Take On The Dalton Conclave
## *May 15–17, 2009*

**Held at the Clear River Teaching Center**
Lynn Hayes, Director

## *(Out-of-the-Box and Off-the-Wall)*

I have decided to end this book by writing "My Take on the Dalton Conclave," as sort of a summarily discourse on where I am on my spirit journey of 79 years. While this report comes out of a *consensus* of collective consciousness, it quite truthfully demonstrates the *positioning* of several of us, myself included. This is the "speaking" of both individuals and the *corporate body* in a right now, contemporary moment as history seems to be headed in the direction of a *cataclysmic fulfillment*. We are literally and figuratively on the brink of a new day in human / divine relationships! The fulfillment of the ages — a NEW AGE! Hence, the title, "My Take on the Dalton Conclave."

"The Heavens Declare" and are declaring the Glory of God! Every day they are speaking profound revelations! They are relevant to the times we are living in. In fact, they are speaking about *right now* events — to be soon culminated in the glorious fulfillment of the ages — of "Peace on Earth, good will to men!"

Hope jumped out at us! Astrology and astronomy confirmed what we already intuitively know deep within our hearts — the earth, sun and stars are already aligned and yet still aligning as we near a climax in the history of men. These thoughts were eloquently shared by Barbara Symons of Texas, as we sat together in heavenly places!

Even the planets are lining up to affect human consciousness toward the "peace and good will" spoken by the prophets, the angels and Jesus!

The Dalton conference pointed out that we, here and now, are also lining up and being conformed to the image of his Son (Our Father) in *unconditional love* — so beautifully expressed by our dear brother, Gary Sigler, who literally and physically glowed in the spirit of love, abounding and transcending! Gary's face shone as he sat amongst us and radiated from deep within the presence of our Heavenly Father!

There were no longer merely concepts of great ideas, but living dynamics permeating the very atmosphere. This was expressed by Annie Ashley in a song, "Your Time Has Come!" Rokus spoke about the new paradigm (perspective) that we all knew in our hearts and is fast coming into fruition!

Amazing! It was like Pentecost, yet much different in form and content as wave after wave of Shekinah Glory filled our hearts with loving praise!

## Oscar Poole

Ruth Minor brought us back into our first estate as we remembered who we really are and remembered each other from former lives!

Prior to the conference I felt anything but spiritual. I had been there only a few minutes when I began to be caught up into higher dimensions. Lynn Hayes called me to the front and after a few stammering words I hit a lick on the piano with a brief rendition of "To God Be The Glory." Something came over and out of me! Music even I had not heard before! As the crowd came to its feet, I witnessed that it was not I playing the piano, but something out of the ordinary had taken place! It was WOW spelled both ways, backward and forward!

To demonstrate how unspiritual I felt before the meeting when Gary Sigler talked about "Potential" on Friday evening, I regressed briefly into a former image of myself — that of a worm! Not an ordinary worm, but a caterpillar worm! I saw myself as having not achieved my *full potential* and that I was only half a caterpillar. I know this is not correct theology, but it is the way I felt! I heard leaves crackling around me as I wiggled around in the earth of my being! I compared the two — my potential and lack of achieving it! For about two months I had been crawling around, when I should have been flying! High above and with the stars that I helped create "back there" somewhere! Up and out of here. My spirit rose immediately as I sat on the edge of my seat!

THERE'S ONLY ONE

## *Elohim*

Did He/She ever speak! Through Lynn Hayes, our host and leader of the conference! Lynn demonstrated his years of the pursuit of truth as he shared from the first three chapters of Genesis. Lynn helped clarify the name of God as Elohim and we saw how we were/are all involved in the creative process.

There were high moments of praise. Loud sounds, low sounds, quiet sounds, relaxing sounds, no sound. But all high frequencies! There were no "Big I's" nor "little you's!" We were all one as we shared together. The atmosphere was charged with life and love — an inclusivity into the one great I AM! We did not need any "burning bushes!" We were all aflame and burned within! We were enlightened with the light from above! In him (and in us, them, they, et. al.) there was no darkness at all! Personally, I felt I was absorbed into the light at the end of the tunnel!

It was a time of great joy, praise — unspeakable and full of glory — it was a celebration!

The conference operated on a *Modus Operandi* of "no preplanned agenda." Lynn simply moderated as the Spirit led in the "now" moments of the weekend.

I think Lynn and I discovered this *agenda-less* way of operation back at Winston-Salem, North Carolina in the fall of 2008 when the spirit moved spontaneously in a motel when a group of us were having breakfast. Barbara Symons appeared on that scene and is now a vital participant in the unfolding drama of these days (the one from College Station, Texas).

Anecdote: As I am bringing this book to a close, though it is open-ended, that is, to be continued, I am writing these closing comments at Valley Forge, Pennsylvania. Edna and I have ridden the AmTrack train for our granddaughter's law degree graduation here at Temple University (Crystal Poole Miller). Trying to bring this timeframe of 79 years to a place to stop — for a while at least.

## *Back to the Dalton Conclave*

Linear and circular time emerged! That we are in a circular, moving of time, which never ends! There is no end, as "what goes around comes around!" (See the book, "Lost Star of Myth & Time" by Walter Cruttenden.) We're in the closing days of an age, not an end in time itself. As Barbara says, "We are connectors between the ages!" I am thankful for this understanding of time and history! We shall never cease to be, but continue on for many ages to come!

Our world shall be saved! Our problems shall be solved! So shall we be as this unfolding drama continues into eternity! What a wonderful way to see and experience life! Eternally now — right here on this planet ship earth as we proceed our sequential orbiting throughout the annals of time ... and eternity!

So, you see, I am concluding my brief span of 79 years on a super positive note! Optimism abounds! Purpose and destiny describes us! We are being aligned with the canon of heaven! Wow! Spell it backwards! It comes out the same!

I believe this Dalton experience was planned for me! Ascended masters, those who have crossed over before us — and many others throughout the universe (or multi-verses) are right now assisting us in achieving the "goals of eternity!"

The Dalton Conclave covered several states: Kansas, Alabama, New York, South Carolina, Georgia, Florida, Texas, Tennessee, North Carolina, Missouri — who knows where else? And this is only the beginning! We are a part of a growing awareness (consciousness) that is sweeping this planet "as the waters cover the sea!" It is truly "world without end" (Isaiah & Paul). We are on a journey.

New metaphors were spoken at the conference in seeking to describe the harmony and syntheses occurring as we spoke. New revelations of life, peace and love are unveiling! As a new wind blows amongst us!

We discovered we are "more than we think we are" — words began to fail to describe what we saw and felt!

Little things became BIG THINGS and vice versa. Everything became and is becoming significant! We basked in our newness and nowness! We laid our heads as it were, on the clouds of heaven and watched the stars as they "danced before us!"

We were truly "outside the box" and "off the wall!" WHAT EXPERIENCES! Over and beyond our wildest imaginations! We felt no need to go to heaven — we were already there! Expanding heavens — even the earth glowed with a new radiance as we glimpsed (took a peek) into the emerging light!

CONVERGENCE and CONFLUENCE described us! There was both a "coming together" and a "going out from" awareness as we soaked in the Spirit as it rained upon us!

Peace, love and good will flowed through us as we became "ONE" with ALL THAT IS!

Others participated: Pat, Evie, George, Carol, Connie, Dorothy, Jim, the Barbara from Indiana, — and a host more whose names slip me! You see, I was "caught up" and became so "other worldly," that I lost sight of many of my surroundings. You might say we were "drugged in the Spirit" or something like that!

We discovered we were on wings "higher than eagles" as we looked down from other dimensions. I think we saw the "Holy City" descending onto earth from out of the heavens! We had a BLAST! Concepts (mere *high sounding* ideas of "right" theologies) became Dynamics! We didn't just talk about love — we became love!

The ESSENCE of God was there because God Himself (and Herself) WAS PRESENT!

And we became ONE!

THERE'S ONLY ONE

Oscar Relaxing at the La Vie Center

Oscar & Edna at the White House Press Room

Oscar Poole

# Addendum IV
# McCutchen-Poole
# Small Business Coalition

**by Al Summers**
Editor, Times-Courier Publishing Co., Inc.
*(Reprinted with permission from Times-Courier Publishing Co., Inc.)*

There is a saying, "There is power in numbers," and two local businessmen are planning to put that idea to work to apply pressure to politicians at all levels to cut wasteful spending and reduce taxes.

Joe McCutchen and Oscar Poole have teamed up to form the Joe McCutchen-Col. Oscar Poole Small Business Coalition where small businesses can band together and present a unified voice when it comes to addressing politicians with regard to laws, especially tax laws, affecting small business owners.

McCutchen explained in most all cities and towns in America, the businesses are considered small businesses, anywhere from a sole proprietorship to a mom-and-pop organization to a business with a handful of employees. Very few large cities have a GM or Ford plant that employs a great number of people.

He uses the Gilmer County community, and the cities of Ellijay and East Ellijay as baseline examples. "We have a large industry here, Pilgrim's Pride, that employs a large number of people. The local plant is owned by a company based in Texas. We have Blueridge Industries, which is owned by a large corporation, and it employs a large number of people. Both would be considered big businesses.

"The school system, which is a government entity, and the local governments employ the next large blocks of employees. Most all of the rest of the businesses you see in town, especially downtown, are small businesses. They outnumber large businesses by a wide margin," he said.

By applying simple mathematics, McCutchen and Poole come up with significant numbers that could, and should, make politicians take a second look at what small business USA is saying.

Said McCutchen, "The key is banding together and showing the political leaders there is a unified front that wishes things to be considered before they enact legislation that affects small business.

Poole says, "We want to rally small business owners for the conservative movement to become a viable force in American politics. I am taking this message to Washington in March to let the politicians know how we feel. It will be in conjunction with my 13th annual 'Take The Pork Back To Washington' trip."

Poole added that a number of politicians have already jumped on the bandwagon with support. "We have both state politicians and national politicians who have endorsed this idea, and we hope to add many more."

Both McCutchen and Poole point to the following statistics and potential, which can be found on Poole's Web site, www.oscarpoole.com.

> 580,000 small businesses in Georgia; 580,000 X 2 = 1.6 million votes; When this army of "small guys" see how important they are, they can be motivated to "get out and vote!"

> The multiplier "2" comes from the fact that most small businesses are owned by two or more people who are also voters. This number could be even higher.

> McCutchen said this is enough votes to sway a primary election in Georgia.

> There are 25 million small businesses in America; 25 x 3 = 75 million votes. Nationwide, on average, there are three owners/employees of voting age associated with each small business. Both men point out that small businesses employ 80 percent of the work force in America.

> While encouraging every small business owner to make their voice heard in both state and national arenas, both men also bring their political views into play by stressing conservatism. They list the following

in implementing their plan for a better future for small business in America:

We want to eliminate the "fat cat" mentality amongst Republicans and focus on the "little guy." We want to demonstrate that sound conservative business principles are the only way to build a strong economy and sustain our American way of life. This is an untapped resource and can revitalize our nation.

We desire to help "little guys" become "big guys"! We want to awaken this "sleeping giant" and forge a new voice in American politics, offsetting left-wing voices of socialism.

We can stimulate the economy from the bottom up and not the top down (which spells disaster!) by lowering taxes, cutting spending, balancing the budget, and reducing government bureaucracy, and encouraging entrepreneurship instead of penalizing it.

Talk-talk-talk; keep the fairness doctrine out. Make use of the media. Everyone keep the calls coming in, realizing power of words.

Let's bring Republicans back to their roots of conservative principles. We can do this by attracting others of like-mind to forge a new collective consciousness of conservatism.

Strong small businesses create jobs, invest in the

economy, and birth new small businesses.

We will revive the American dream and give rise to a new wave of prosperity.

We will inspire new ideas in the marketplace and give rise to a new prosperity.

Both men want to make Gilmer County the center of small business promotion, and what started with the idea of two is beginning to grow.

There is power in numbers.

**www.oscarpoole.com**
E-mail: oscarpoole@aol.com

# *Breaking News!*

Just as this book is going to press the following news from Washington:

The "Club for Growth," the congressional scorecard, which rates the voting of members of congress regarding *conservative* values, reveals that Georgia is NUMBER ONE in the nation with six members scoring above 90!

Could it be that our coalition is already having an impact?!

There's Only One

Oscar, Mitt Romney, and Edna

Edna, Zell Miller, Oscar

OSCAR POOLE

# Addendum V

## GILMER COUNTY
### BOARD OF COMMISSIONERS

1 Broad St. Suite 106, Ellijay, GA 30540
P: 706-635-4361 F: 706-635-4351
Comment Line: 706-515-2320
WWW.GILMERCOUNTY-GA.GOV

WILL BEATTIE, *Commissioner, Post 1* | DAVID CLARK, *County Attorney*
MARK CHASTAIN, *Chairman* | JC SANFORD, *Commissioner, Post 2* | FAYE HARVEY, *Financial Officer* | DIANA BUTTRAM, *County Clerk*

Entering the small, Southern community of Gilmer County you will first notice the innate natural beauty of the illustrious mountains, tall hemlocks, and grazing pigs. Grazing pigs!? Yes, one of the nations's most forward thinking entrepreneurs decided to give a touch of culture to the business scene. Exploring marketing ideas like placing a "signature pig" with your name on it and staking it to the side of the mountain. As the news of the delicious BB-Q spred, so did the herd. Today, you notice nearly 4,000 of "grazing pigs" that dot the mountainscape behind and around the location of the famous Poole's BB-Q on the "Pig Hall of Fame".

Oscar Poole is not only a marketing genius but he gives true meaning to what this nation was founded upon….."Entrepreneurial spirit". With his funny yellow suit and decorated cars, he has made quite a name for himself. His bold antics of "taking the pork back to Washington" has given conservative humor and won Oscar's place in the heart of many national politicians.

Because of Oscar's iconic success the reputation of Poole's BB-Q goes unmatched by many other small businesses. Numerous Senators, Congressmen, Governors, State Representatives and local politicians have held the location for rally's, events, meet and greets, and the like. However, it is not the location alone that is the attraction, it is a small business success story that sets the tone for conservative political thought and a positive outlook on what can happen when you have a plan and the desire to succeed.

I have been both honored to know Colonel Oscar Poole and inspired to achieve great things by his commitment to his faith, family, and Country.

Sincerely,

Commissioner Will Beattie
Gilmer County, GA Board of Commissioners

## Addendum VI

THERE'S ONLY ONE

GILMER COUNTY CHAMBER OF COMMERCE
706.635.7400
706.635.7410 Fax
WWW.GILMERCHAMBER.COM

MAILING ADDRESS:
PO BOX 505
ELLIJAY, GA 30540

PHYSICAL ADDRESS:
368 CRAIG STREET
EAST ELLIJAY, GA 30539

Colonel Oscar Poole
P.O. Box 690
East Ellijay, GA 305039

Dear Colonel Poole,

I can't tell you what an honor it is for me to be included in your broad circle of friends. However, I can say it is hard to resist your kindness, openness, and of course your energy.

Being a relatively new Gilmer County resident, I still remember the first day I drove into town to start my job at the Chamber of Commerce. Of course my eyes were immediately drawn to the Pig Hill of Fame on my right as I drove in. My first thought was, "Wow! Now, I've got to meet the man behind that!" Little did I know that behind those pigs was an incredible salesman and an even more incredible friend to the community.

Your current undertaking in helping make Gilmer County the "Small Business Capital of the World" is very close to my heart, and one that I give my full support to. Small business owners are the heart and backbone of this country. They are our past, present and future.

I celebrate with you on the publication of your most recent book. I am sure it will tell your story as only you can with humility and humor. Your pursuit and capturing of the American Dream is an inspiring story to all Americans. It reminds us that we all have special gifts and we just have to be the best we can be.

Again, thank you for welcoming me and more importantly thank you for just being you.

Congratulations!

Warmest Regards,

*Paige*

Paige Green, President
Gilmer County Chamber of Commerce


P.S. And the BBQ isn't too bad either!

OSCAR POOLE

# Addendum VII

## City of East Ellijay

Mack G. West
Mayor

Mitzi L. Darnell
City Clerk

*107 Oak Street*
*P. O. Box 1060*
*East Ellijay, GA 30539*
*Phone (706) 276 - 3111*
*Fax (706) 276 - 3112*

Councilmembers
Donald Callihan
Fred Keener
Gene McClure
James Sellers

---

June 8, 2009

Oscar & Edna Poole
164 Craig Street
East Ellijay, Georgia

Dear Neighbors,

Having recently learned of your retirement, I just wanted to express my sincere gratitude for all you have done for the City of East Ellijay.

I vividly recall our first meeting in 1989 when Oscar came by City Hall to acquire a business license for a "portable barbecue stand" on Craig Street. As the site was located in a transitional neighborhood consisting of several dilapidated one-family residences, the City Council felt that a commercial endeavor in this area might encourage landowners to participate in our urban renewal efforts. Lo and behold, that is exactly what has happened in recent years!

As the business evolved over the years, through your coordinated efforts and innovative ideas such as the Hill-of-Fame, Taj-Ma-Hog, and the Pig Mobile, the little trailer/shack was eventually replaced by a permanent cabin type structure.

On many occasions over the years, I have referred to Col. Poole as our City's one man Chamber of Commerce. In hundreds of articles in National and statewide publications as well as on your TV and radio appearances, Col Poole's unique BBQ Shack was always "geographically located" in East Ellijay, Georgia. You have done more that any individual, living or dead, to put our City on the map.

Several years ago, while traveling in Europe, my wife and I were seated in a café in London at Victoria Station. Along came a traveler proudly sporting one of your T-shirts. We were amazed at this occurrence and upon questioning, the gent related that he had dined at your restaurant the previous day. He was extremely complimentary of the food and the uniqueness of your establishment.

Oscar, I am happy for both you and Edna. Your personal lives have been an inspiration to many. May God bless you in your golden years. The success of your business endeavor from a very humble beginning in a small town in North Georgia makes me proud to be an American.

Kindest personal regards,

*Mack G. West*

Mack G. West, Mayor

THERE'S ONLY ONE

# Addendum VIII

## Congressional Record
United States of America
PROCEEDINGS AND DEBATES OF THE *106th* CONGRESS, FIRST SESSION

THURSDAY, MAY 27, 1999

## *Senate*
### TRIBUTE TO TEN YEARS OF SERVING THE SOUTH'S FINEST BARBEQUE

Mr. COVERDELL. Mr. President, I rise today to commend Mr. Oscar Poole, affectionately known as "Colonel" in the north Georgia town of Ellijay, who on June 4th will be celebrating his tenth year of business as one of our great state's foremost authorities on barbecue. Throughout his ten years of service in this little town resting in the scenic foothills of the Appalachian Mountains, Colonel Poole has served customers both far and wide, from nearly every state in the Union, and more than several countries.

The grassy embankment behind this now landmark establishment, pays tribute to the many thousands of customers that have passed through the town of Ellijay to eat the Colonel's barbecue. The embankment, referred to as the "Pig Hill of Fame," is covered by nearly 4,000 personalized, painted, and pig shaped signs. Individuals, families, tour groups, friends, Sunday school classes, and celebrities have each had pigs erected to memorialize their visit to one of the South's greatest places for barbecue. In fact, I am fortunate enough to have a sign in my name on this famed hill. As many in the South know, politics and barbecue go hand in hand. Therefore, it comes as no surprise to learn that governors, congressmen, Senators, statesmen, and even Presidential candidates have made the voyage to Colonel Poole's.

Colonel Poole's reputation supersedes our state's boundaries. On three separate occasions he was the highlight of Capitol Hill. On his first trip to Washington, the Colonel arrived at the steps of the Capitol in his large yellow Pig Mobile and in his colorful and patriotic suit to deliver his hickory smoked pork to the entire Georgia delegation and their staffs. Much to the dismay of some in the delegation, word about real Georgia barbecue got around Washington so fast that the Colonel's rations, enough for 450 people, quickly ran out. On another occasion, I had the opportunity to serve what may be one of Georgia's finest kept secrets to several of my friends and colleagues here in the Senate who meet for a weekly lunch.

While most know the Colonel as a barbecue maestro, he is a wearer of many hats. His customers know he is also a pianist. Others know of him as a preacher. This man with a big heart is all of these things and more.

Inside his tin covered, pine wood restaurant the Colonel plays classical music, show tunes, and almost every customer request. Having learned to play the piano at an early age, Mr. Poole has long since appreciated his gift as a musician. His ability to play was good enough to put himself through the Methodist seminary where he was ordained a minister.

His work in the Church, as a preacher and a missionary, took him to many rural communities here in the South and to developing countries like Brazil. It was this sort of compassion that enabled a north Georgia gentleman named Wendell Cross to approach the Colonel for instruction on how to read. Mr. Cross, a sixty year old man, had spent his entire life not knowing how to read. That was until Mr. Poole took him under his wing and worked with him on a daily basis for nearly twelve months. Eventually Mr. Cross learned to read. The story of compassion and friendship received nationwide media coverage and was shown on the popular "Today Show."

More importantly, two days before the tenth anniversary of his business, Colonel Poole will be celebrating his 49th, I repeat, 49th year of marriage to his lovely wife, Edna Poole. This is a milestone that anyone would be extremely proud, and I am happy to report that the Poole's will have four sons...Michael, Greg, Keith, and Darvin...to help them celebrate this milestone.

Once again, Mr. President, I would like to commend Colonel Oscar Poole on his tenth year of business and his 49th year of marriage. During this time when there are discussions of the direction of today's culture, Colonel Poole is an example of how leading one's life by a core set of good, American values...faith, family, and country...will result in a life of many successes.

OSCAR POOLE

# Addendum IX

**OFFICE OF LIEUTENANT GOVERNOR**
240 STATE CAPITOL
ATLANTA, GEORGIA 30334

CASEY CAGLE
LIEUTENANT GOVERNOR

August 8, 2007

Colonel Poole
164 Craig Street
East Ellijay GA 30539

Dear Colonel Poole,

Thank you very much for inviting me to share lunch with you at Poole's Famous BBQ. I enjoyed seeing you and truly appreciate the time I spent in Ellijay.

You have done a wonderful job building a business from the ground up and are an example to many.

My door is always open to you, and I hope you will contact me if I can be of service.

Sincerely,

Casey Cagle
Lt. Governor of Georgia

CC/jh

# Addendum X

**SAXBY CHAMBLISS**
GEORGIA

United States Senate
Washington, D.C.

13 August, 2007

Oscar & Edna,

Many thanks for staying late on Friday evening so we could enjoy the world's Best Bar-B-Que. Enjoyed our visit & look forward to seeing you again soon.

Saxby

# Other Works by Col. Poole

### Books
Speak-To-It!
God in the Marketplace
How To Make Things Happen
The Physics of Spirit
Col. Poole's Core Beliefs
I Hear Music!

### Videos
Col. Poole's Secrets of Success

### CDs
Col. Poole's Favorites
The Sound of Music
To God Be The Glory
Camp Meeting Melodies
Glory To His Name
Christmas in the North Georgia Mountains

### Web Sites
www.oscarpoole.com
www.poolesbarbq.com
www.wcba.tv
www.laviecenter.org

THERE'S ONLY ONE

John McCain and Oscar Poole

Oscar Poole with Mr. and Mrs. Mitt Romney

Oscar Poole with Governor Sonny Perdue

THERE'S ONLY ONE

Oscar and Edna Poole with Miss America; Heather Whitestone

Oscar on the set with Cherie Martin – *North Ga. Now Today*

## Oscar Poole

Cynthia and Reggie Johnson – Oscar Poole

Oscar and Lt. Gov. Casey Cagle, GA

There's Only One

Oscar and Clint Day

Oscar and John Oxendine

- 306 -

# Oscar Poole

Oscar attending the Republic National Convention; New York 2004

THERE'S ONLY ONE

Col. Oscar Poole has been featured on the
front page cover of Roll Call

Oscar fed over 400 Congressmen and their staff members
in the Sam Rayburn Building.

# Oscar Poole

There's Only One Oscar Poole

THERE'S ONLY ONE

Oscar Enjoying LIFE!

OSCAR POOLE

## **A Note from the Publisher**

Oscar Poole is certainly one of the 'hidden mysteries' of the conservative movement today. His refreshing outlook and solutions proposed are what is desperately needed from local school governments to Washington, D.C. He has maintained the 'true' conservative philosophy that has been lost on most media 'bloviators' and mouthpieces of the Republican Party.

His views, if immediately embraced, could be the saving grace for the GOP and the entire conservative movement. History supports the 'true' conservative philosophy and is the reason that conservative Democrats held rule over the South for over 100 years. It was not the party, but the philosophy of conservative, limited, and restrained government.

TGS would probably be considered a 'liberal' publisher, because the media thinks they must 'label' everyone and everything into identifiable camps, thus aiding and abetting the political parties to divide and conquer the people of America.

Having had several conversations with Oscar Poole during the development of this book, I find there is little difference in his conservative goals and my so-called liberal goals. Additionally, our approach to solutions is virtually the same. As small business owners, we both identify such things as NAFTA and GATT as major obstacles to free and fair trade WITHIN THE USA. Both of us oppose big business corporations ruling over the entire financial and economic world, through the power of money, greed, and corruption.

> Basically
> the people are RIGHT,
> the parties are WRONG
> the government is WRONG.

So in the conservative movement and the GOP there really is ONLY ONE OSCAR POOLE that is speaking out against the abuses of the entrenched over-reaching government interference in our lives and businesses. In the world of Georgian BBQ, again THERE IS ONLY ONE OSCAR POOLE.

Liberal or Conservative you've got to meet the one and only Oscar Poole and let his common sense open your eyes to common ground and viable solutions to repair America.

L. Savage
TGS Publishing

There's Only One

### Hidden Mysteries

## *TGS Publishers*

## 22241 Pinedale Lane
## Frankston, Texas 75763

HiddenMysteries.com

903-876-3256

Wholesale and Retail